GAELIC INFLUENCE IN ICELAND

GÍSLI SIGURÐSSON

GAELIC INFLUENCE IN ICELAND

HISTORICAL AND LITERARY CONTACTS

A SURVEY OF RESEARCH

**SECOND EDITION
WITH A NEW INTRODUCTION**

UNIVERSITY OF ICELAND PRESS
REYKJAVÍK 2000

ISBN: 9979-54-434-1

CONTENTS

PREFACE

This book was written in Dublin and presented to the National University of Ireland in June 1986 in fulfilment of the thesis requirement for the degree of Master of Philosophy in Medieval Studies. It was later published, in 1988, as volume 46 in the *Studia Islandica* series at the University of Iceland, edited by Sveinn Skorri Höskuldsson.

The main chapters are now published again, unaltered, but with a new preface and a new general introduction. This includes information on the historical background of the westward expansion of the Vikings, and an overview of literary activities in Iceland during the middle ages.

In the 1980s, it was still considered almost taboo in Icelandic studies to take up the old issue of the Gaelic influence on Icelandic tradition, to view Icelandic culture in the settlement period as a melting pot of Norse and Gaelic elements. Many scholars in the field are still inclined to ignore this aspect of Icelandic culture (as can be seen from the fact that no Icelandic journal published a review of the first edition of this book though several foreign ones did, even as far south as Italy; also, that at a conference arranged by the Icelandic Science Society in 1990 — the proceedings of which were published as *Um landnám á Íslandi* in 1996 — this was not even considered an issue). Instead they focus on the established continental contacts that were built up through the institutional network of the Roman church in the high Middle Ages, about which we have contemporary written sources.

In spite of that general trend, several works have appeared since this book was first published which have concentrated on not only Viking and Gaelic contacts in the British Isles but also Gaelic cultural impact on Icelandic tradition. A few can be mentioned here to give readers an idea of the scope of these studies, and to orient them towards more recent works: Bo Almqvist's important article from 1996 on Gaelic/Norse folklore contacts which appeared in the volume *Irland und Europa im früheren Mittelalter*; the proceedings from the fourth symposium of Societas Celtologica Nordica which appeared in 1997 under the title *Celts and Vikings,* edited by Folke Josephson; *Vikings in Scotland,* by James Graham-Campbell and Colleen E. Batey, from 1998; and the book *Ireland and Scandinavia in the Early Viking Age*, edited by Howard B. Clarke, Máire Ní Mhaonaigh and Raghnall Ó Floinn, also published in 1998. Additionally, since that time, two Icelandic books have also appeared on this theme: *Keltar á Íslandi* by Hermann Pálsson which came out in 1996, and Helgi Guðmundsson's book from 1997, *Um haf innan*, which takes a somewhat different approach to the subject (see my review of it in *Alvíssmál* 9, 1999: 109-111).

The field of genetic studies, discussed in chapter 3 of the present work, has changed radically since the 1980s, making the strong reaction from Stefán Aðalsteinsson (see the 1989, 1990, 1992 and 1993 volumes of the Icelandic journal *Saga*, with both his contributions and my responses/corrections) on that front more or less obsolete. The reader may be guided to an article by Jeff T. Williams, "Origin and Population Structure of the Icelanders" in *Human Biology*, April 1993, and to the ongoing research by Agnar Helgason et al. (e.g. in *American Journal of Human Genetics* 66 and 67, 2000) which suggests that among the first settlers in Iceland, a much larger proportion of women than men came from the Gaelic world (his tentative conclusions at present are that more than 50% of the women and about 20% of the men may have been Gaelic). Agnar Helgason's conclusions bring to mind that in addition to the nationalistic dimension of the denial of the Gaelic element in Iceland, we may also have a 'muted' gender-related problem on our hands.

I would like to repeat my thanks from the first publication of this work to the following persons who were all of great help to me during the writing of this book: the late David A. H. Evans, University

College Dublin, who supplied me with numerous offprints and photocopies of relevant material; Bo Almqvist, U.C.D. (now emeritus), whom I could consult at all times, and who drew my attention to many items which would otherwise have gone unnoticed as well as advising me on the usage of the English language; Charles Doherty, U.C.D., who kindly read the chapters on Viking contacts and the Gaels in Iceland in draft form, giving me some sound advice; Patrick F. Wallace, now director of the National Museum of Ireland, who was also kind enough to read the same chapters and correct some of my mistakes in interpreting the archaeological evidence; the biologists, Jón Magnús Einarsson, and Anna Kristín Daníelsdóttir, both doctoral students at U.C.D. at the time, who instructed me in genealogical terminology and read the chapter on blood groups; Tomás Ó Cathasaigh, U.C.D. (now at Harvard), who was kind enough to read through a draft of the book and assist me in finding various references; the writer Eilís Ní Dhuibhne who corrected and improved my English; and Honóra Ní Chríogáin, who used to be a secretary in the Old Irish Department in U.C.D., without whose continual cheering and support in my dealings with both Irish and Icelandic bureaucracy this work would never have been written; and finally, to the numerous other individuals who were, throughout the writing process, willing to discuss and share their thoughts with me on the problem of Gaelic-Icelandic contacts. In addition to the above, I want to thank those who have invited me to air my views on Gaelic influence in Iceland, both in public lectures and in media-programs: Andrés Eiríksson; Þorvaldur Friðriksson; Ragnheiður Gyða Jónsdóttir; Mímir, the union of students in Icelandic studies at the University of Iceland; the University of Manitoba; the University of Akureyri; the University of Turku and the Finnish Society for Celtic Studies; and the University of Basel. Not least was it inspiring to be able to benefit from Stephen N. Tranter's company and studies on the comparative aspect of the poetic traditions during my sabbatical in 1995, as a guest of the research project: *Übergänge und Spannungsfelder zwischen Mündlichkeit und Schriftlichkeit* at the University of Freiburg im Breisgau. Most recently, I have been encouraged by the iv

ongoing research and activity of Thomas J. Martin who has put tremendous effort into increasing the general awareness in the Irish American community of this aspect of the cultural contribution of their ancestors. Last, but not least, special thanks are due to Barbara B. Nelson for her thorough and careful editing of the introduction to the second edition of this work.

Primary sources which are mentioned in the text are listed in the bibliography, where information on the editions used may be found. Page and chapter numbers refer to these editions. In order to make the bibliography more useful, I have included works in a separate section, called *Further Reading*. These works are not referred to, specifically, in the text: some of them I have consulted, others only looked at in passing, and some came to my attention too late to be included in my discussion. Non-English quotations from scholarly works are translated by me; for texts, I have used published translations, which are identified in each case.

Reykjavík, October 2000
Gísli Sigurðsson

INTRODUCTION

Great events first become noteworthy when someone tells their story. In the Middle Ages the Icelanders drew on their oral lore to create literary works which contained memories from the Viking Age (800-1050). These describe a time when the peoples of Scandinavia used their superior ships to win power and influence across the Baltic Sea and into Russia, even as far south as the Caspian Sea and Constantinople. They also crossed the North Sea to the British Isles and Ireland where they established colonies in Dublin, York and the Orkneys. Eventually they reached the Faroe Islands and Iceland in the North Atlantic, both of which had been visited sporadically by Irish hermits. After their country had been settled for about one hundred years, the Icelanders continued on to Greenland and then to the North American continent, where they named the territories they found, from north to south: *Helluland* (Slab-stone land), *Markland* (Forest land) and *Vínland* (Land of grapes). This all took place in just over two hundred years from the first attack by Norwegian seafarers on the monastery of Lindisfarne off the east coast of England in 793, an event which is generally considered to mark the start of the Viking Age. The Vikings were fearsome warriors who combined their lust for trade and warfare with a quest for new lands which they explored, settled and ruled. Their scope for expansion seemed almost limitless until they were finally outnumbered by the natives in North America a thousand years ago. After a few years of attempting settlement, they took to the sea again, thus postponing European influence in North America for another five hundred years.

Viking activity in the west

The Viking raid on the monastery at Lindisfarne in 793 ushered in a great period of hostilities in western Europe. Danes burned down Dorestad, a major French port, four times during the period 834-837, and in 845, Ragnar *loðbrók* led 120 ships which sailed up the Seine, sacked Rouen and Paris, and held them ransom until King Charles the Bald of France paid him 7000 pounds of silver. Vikings first wintered on the continent in 842-843, at Noirmoutier on the Loire estuary, which was the centre of the salt and wine trade. Björn *járnsíða*, Ragnar *loðbrók*'s son, raided on the Seine in 856-857 and, in 859, set off with his companion Hástein on a four-year voyage of war with 62 ships in the Mediterranean, the greatest known Viking expedition of the ninth century. They were headed for Rome, but mistakenly sacked Luna in north Italy instead. On their way back, they were ambushed by Moors at Gibraltar and only 20 ships returned to Noirmoutier in 862. Danes led by Göngu-Hrólfur settled in Normandy after making a treaty with the King of France in 911, and in 1066 their descendants, led by William the Conqueror (known in Icelandic sources as Vilhjálmur *bastarður*), invaded and conquered England.

Early in the Viking Age, Danes began to settle in the north and east of England, in the region which came to be known as the Danelaw. In 865, three sons of Ragnar (possibly *loðbrók*, who sacked Paris in 845), named Hálfdan, Ubbi and Ívar *beinlausi*, attacked England, capturing York in November 866. Ásbjartur and Ella, who had ruled York, tried to recapture it the following spring, but were both killed. Ívar, who had gone to York from Ireland and returned there afterwards, died in Dublin in 873 as "King of the Northerners in Ireland and Britain." According to the *Saga of Ragnar loðbrók*, after King Ella killed Ragnar in a pit of snakes, Ragnar's sons arrived from Denmark to avenge him by "carving a blood-eagle" on Ella — cutting his lungs out from the back. In England, a similar tale is told of King Edmund of East Anglia, who was killed by Danish invaders in 870. York was under Danish rule until 919, when Rögnvaldur, a Norwegian from Dublin, gained control of it. King Athelstan of Wessex drove Olaf Sigtryggsson and King Gudfred of Dublin out of York in

927, but Olaf Gudfredsson went there from Dublin in 939, and held the town until 944. Eiríkur *blóðöx* was the last Viking king to rule York, from 948-954.

Around 800, Scandinavians settled in Shetland and the Orkneys, where Picts and Celts were living, some as monks or missionaries. Hrafna-Flóki stopped in Shetland en route to the Faroe Islands and thence to Iceland in the middle of the 9th century, and many powerful Norwegians fled to the Scottish islands — Shetland, the Orkneys and the Hebrides — to escape King Haraldur *hárfagri*, who himself is said to have raided Shetland near the end of the 9th century and given it to Earl Rögnvaldur of Mæri, together with the Orkneys. *Egils saga*, *Njáls saga* and *Fljótsdæla saga* mention sailing from Shetland to Iceland, and King Ólafur Tryggvason of Norway is said to have Christianised Shetland and the Orkneys in 1000, although archaeologists now consider that the Scandinavians there became Christian much earlier. The Earls of Orkney ruled Shetland until King Sverrir Sigurðsson of Norway incorporated it into his realm in 1195. The Faroe Islands and Shetland maintained close contact in the Middle Ages; all Shetland place names are of Nordic origin and a Nordic language, Norn, was spoken there until the 18th century. Well-preserved Viking Age ruins, known as Jarlshof, are found on the southern side of the main island, but the main port is thought to have been on the west, at Papa Stour, since there are persistent fogs to the east of the islands and dangerous waters to the south, through the Ness Yoal. Both *Orkneyinga saga* and *Hákonar saga* mention lives being lost there.

The Orkneys became the centre for Viking expeditions to the northern part of the British Isles and an important link between the Gaelic and Nordic cultures. For example, Orkney Islanders fought in the Battle of Clontarf in 1014, and joined Haraldur *harðráði*'s attack on England in 1066. The Orkneys feature widely in the Icelandic *Landnámabók*, the *Book of Settlements* (the foremost woman settler, Auður *djúpúðga*, stopped there on her way from Dublin to Iceland, for example), and also in the *Íslendingasögur*, but it is *Orkneyinga saga* which is our main written source of Viking Age history there, focusing on the earls who reigned over it.

Caithness, in northern Scotland was settled by Scandinavians after Viking earls conquered the Orkneys. Vikings established themselves early on in the Hebrides, and Haraldur *hárfagri* is said to have raided there. He did not manage to keep the Hebrides, however, so he "sent Ketill *flatnefur*, son of Björn Buna, to the west to win back the islands. Ketill sailed west, conquered all the Hebrides and became chieftain over them." Vikings repeatedly attacked the monastery on the sacred island of Iona in the Hebrides in the early ninth century, burning and pillaging it, until the monks fled to Kells in Ireland (after which the Book of Kells is named). By the tenth century, however, the Scandinavian community in Dublin was firmly Christian, and Ólafur Kvaran, king there from 953, died on a pilgrimage to Iona in 981.

Vikings came to the Isle of Man in the ninth century and established a community with its own parliament at Tynwald, which was under Scandinavian rule until the thirteenth century. From a ninth-century heathen burial mound we can tell that a female sacrifice was made at the funeral of a Scandinavian chieftain, but by the tenth century the Manx settlement had become Christian. Many relics and place names testify to Scandinavian rule on the Isle of Man.

The Vikings began their raids on Ireland in 795 and continued them, with increasing frequency, as the ninth century progressed, both by the coast and along rivers deep inland. After 840 they settled in Ireland, building towns and fortresses on the east and south coasts as bases for launching raids. They gradually accepted Christianity and adapted to Irish society, taking part in domestic power struggles such as the Battle of Clontarf in 1014, in which Scandinavians fought on both sides. Scandinavian influence persisted in Ireland until the twelfth century. In 841, Vikings founded Dublin on the banks of the Liffey. Ólafr *hvíti*, possibly the husband of Auður *djúpúðga*, was king of the Vikings there in the mid-ninth century; he was succeeded by Ívar *beinlausi*, who reigned until 873. Dublin became the centre of the viking slave trade which flourished in 869 and the following decades, judging by references in the Irish annals. At the same time, the raids by invading armies on Ireland stopped, leading to what was known as the "40-year peace" around the time Iceland was being settled. The Vikings were driven out of Dublin in 902, but by 917 they had returned and resumed their earlier business. It is thought that their slave trade was not only directed towards Iceland and mainland Scandinavia, but also extended south to the Mediterranean.

On September 25, 1066, King Haraldur *harðráði* of Norway was killed, along with many of his troops, in the Battle of Stamford Bridge against King Harold Godwinson. Both were contesting the throne of England after the death of Edward the Confessor. Only 19 days later, William the Conqueror and his Norman army defeated Harold's exhausted troops at the Battle of Hastings. Over the following years William fought not only domestic unrest but also aggression by the Danes, who attacked England for the last time in 1085, led by Canute II (St. Canute).

The Settlement of Iceland

Our main sources of information about the settlement of Iceland are Icelandic writings, supplemented by both archaeological evidence and the writings of foreign historians. Strong doubts have sometimes been raised about the credibility of Icelandic works from the twelfth and thirteenth centuries — *Íslendingabók*, the *Book of Icelanders*, and *Landnámabók*, the *Book of Settlements* — given that they describe events supposed to have taken place two to four centuries earlier. However, when Christianity brought literacy to Iceland, medieval historians necessarily sought information about the past in oral stories and lore.

Living oral traditions studied in many parts of the world have shown a tendency to adapt to contemporary reality, whereby facts change according to the context in which they are repeated, even though people consider themselves to be preserving memories from the past. Despite this mutability, however, it is still possible to talk about a continuous tradition lasting several centuries and embodying essential truths which are archaeologically verifiable. For example, we know that the written accounts are correct insofar as they claim that Iceland was rapidly settled after 870 by people from Norway and

Britain, with several hundred large estates owned by chieftains and some three thousand farms. This dating can be ascertained from the "Settlement Layer" of volcanic ash which covered a large part of the country following an eruption in 871 (± 1 year), as may be corroborated by ice core samples from the Greenland glacier. Immediately above this layer of ash are relics of the oldest settlements in Iceland. The saga writers and chroniclers also knew that people left Iceland to settle in Greenland near the end of the tenth century. Likewise they knew stories about sailing to the continent of North America around 1000 — as was confirmed when relics left by people from Greenland and Iceland were found in the 1960s at L'Anse aux Meadows on the northern point of Newfoundland. The saga writers knew that heathendom was the prevailing faith during the settlement of Iceland, and that Christianity was adopted by law around 1000. All this was known because people preserved the memories of these events, told stories about them and linked the names and lineage of certain individuals to specific incidents. It is an inherent feature of narrative art and the oral tradition that various details inevitably stray from the straight and narrow path of truth on their long journey through the centuries. Inconsistencies in detail, however, do not alter the overall picture presented, which is well compatible with archaeological findings.

Many of the settlers of Iceland were Christian, even though Scandinavian culture and heathendom prevailed at first after the settlement. People of Scandinavian descent were in charge of administration, as well as farming and other work, and provided the crafts and skills, household articles and domestic animals by which society was sustained. Slaves were given Scandinavian names and had to learn the language of their masters, so their culture was never dominant. Although it is impossible to assess the distribution of different religions in the ninth and tenth centuries, archaeological finds tell us that the Scandinavians in Shetland and Orkney had adopted Christianity long before the end of the tenth century when, according to written sources, King Ólafur Tryggvason is supposed to have converted them. The people who left Breiðafjörður in Iceland with Eiríkur *rauði* in 985 or 986 and settled in Greenland did not leave behind any signs of heathen burial customs in that country. The oldest graves in the cemetery of Þjóðhildur's church in Brattahlíð in the eastern settlement are Christian, and date from the end of the tenth century. This shows that Christianity was the living religion of these people, even though Ólafur Tryggvason is supposed to have sent Leifur Eiríksson (Leifur *heppni*) to convert them in 1000. Many of the settlers around Breiðafjörður are said to have originally come from the Gaelic world, and are thus likely to have brought the Christian faith to Iceland with them when they arrived.

Early on in the settlement period, Iceland was divided not only into geographically delimited parishes, but also into chieftaincies (*goðorð*) which did not depend on where people lived. *Goðar* had both a religious and a secular administrative function. District assemblies were held regularly and when the general assembly or *Alþingi* was established at Þingvellir in 930, chieftains began convening there once a year to consult, make laws and pass judgements about disputes. Implementation of sentences was generally on the initiative of the *goðar* and not any central executive power. Around the time of the establishment of the *Alþingi*, Iceland's population would have been between 10 and 20 thousand. There were 36 *goðorð* at first, but their number was increased to 39 and the country was divided into four quarters under a legal reform in 965. Three assemblies were then held in each quarter, except in the north, where there were four. A law speaker, responsible for preserving the law, was chosen at the *Alþingi* for a term of three years. His function was to recite the law, which was preserved orally until the introduction of writing, and also to rule on disputes about interpretations of it. Many of the sagas hinge on the way personal disputes overlapped with the legal authority of the *goðar* and *Alþingi*. Tension often developed between the ancient duty of revenge and the sentences imposed under the rule of law, leading to escalating feuds and bloody conflict which could only be conciliated by the new Christian philosophy of peace and forgiveness.

The people who lived around Breiðafjörður undoubtedly knew the tales from Ireland about fantastic countries to the west, lands of plenty where the Irish envisaged beautiful women, endless wine, rivers full of huge salmon, and eternal bliss. These highly fanciful stories resemble Viking notions of *Ódáinsvellir* (the Plains of the Undead) insofar as those who go to this paradise have no way of returning to their earthly lives. Accounts in the *Landnámabók* and later sources about Ari Másson and other people from Breiðafjörður reaching the "Land of the White Men" could be an offshoot of these legends, and it is not improbable that such stories may have encouraged people to sail and search for land to the west. When Eiríkur *rauði* went to settle in Greenland, for example, a Christian from the Hebrides is mentioned as accompanying him. After people from Iceland and Greenland had travelled all the way to the North American mainland where the flora and climate resembled the descriptions in these legends, it is not unlikely that fact and fiction merged, leading people to believe they had actually reached the countries with which they were already familiar from these stories.

Eddas and sagas in a cultural melting pot
Iceland's claim to fame in the intellectual world is based on its medieval literature. This literature laid the foundation for many of Iceland's arguments during the struggle for independence in the 19th and early 20th centuries; it justified our claim to nationhood, and was used to show that we spoke a different language, a language that we had preserved remarkably well since the Middle Ages. Our medieval literature served as proof that we had created something unique, something which made us different from the rest of Scandinavia. This heritage is also said to have kept us alive through the ages, to have given us the self-confidence to face the world proudly and say, "Here you can see how great and glorious our forefathers were" — assuming, of course, that some of the glory stuck to us, the descendants!

But what are we talking about when we boast of the Icelandic literary heritage? The key words are *Eddas* and *Sagas*, all written in the Icelandic vernacular, which we can still read today without too much difficulty. The fact that Latin was not our literary language sets these works in a class with the Irish sagas, the only other secular heroic prose literature of its type in this part of the world, which was written in the vernacular. In Norway, written literature of the time was of a religious and courtly nature, consisting mostly of translations of foreign works.

People from Iceland made a name for themselves as poets at the royal courts in Scandinavia and the British Isles, composing, for the most part, poetic encomia in an exceptionally complicated metre called "skaldic metre." The study and art of skaldic poetry — which has a special vocabulary for the most frequently used terms in the genre (e.g., kings, warriors, battles, swords, spears, bows, arrows, ships, sails, oars, women) — is the subject of a book written by Iceland's most renowned writer during its literary Golden Age in the 13th century, Snorri Sturluson. Called *Snorra Edda*, the book gathers together all the traditional oral learning that professional poets had to acquire in order to be able to compose verse in skaldic metre. This learning consisted in large part of pagan myths that form the basis of our knowledge of old Norse mythology, upon which the poetic circumlocutions, called *kennings*, are mostly based. In other words, the old pagan myths are the frame of reference for the poetic language of the skaldic poems. In a Christian 13th century, this seems to have caused Snorri some problems, as he makes formal excuses at the beginning of the book, explaining that these stories do not tell of real gods — even though people used to think so. He then proceeds to relate all the myths as he learned them, in prose and poetry. He explains the pagan cosmology and describes the beginning of the world and its structure by recounting myths that refer to the earth and the sky above us. Towards the end he composes his own poem of praise, using all the phraseology that he has introduced, and presenting all possible variants of the standard skaldic metre.

Needless to say, Snorri's book is our main source for the oral lore and myths of old, which professional poets had to master long after the introduction of Christianity. These myths were still kept alive in the 13th century, as the writing of *Snorra Edda* will attest, even though they must have been on the decline at that time. Part of the wisdom was presented in the same way as was common practice in contemporary Latin books of learning, such as *Elucidarius*, in which the disciple asks his master questions. However, from the way that most of the material is presented and analysed, it is clear that Snorri is firmly grounded in a native tradition of learning, in which poets and scholars have obviously thought systematically about the art of poetry.

Presumably the old lore and knowledge was widespread in Scandinavia during the pagan Viking Age, but it was in Iceland that it was cultivated and developed, and, in the 13th century, finally written down. This Icelandic book is therefore a major contribution to the preservation of this ancient learning.

More traditional oral poems containing pagan myths and heroic lore common to Scandinavia and even, more widely, to the old Germanic cultural area of North-western Europe, were also kept alive in Iceland much longer than elsewhere, and were eventually put into writing in the 13th century. These are the so-called *eddaic poems*, which differ from skaldic poems in content: they deal with gods and half-divine heroes rather than with human kings. The metre and poetic diction of the eddaic poems are much simpler and easier to understand than those of skaldic poetry; indeed, they are very much like the metre and diction of the Old English *Beowulf* and the Old High German *Hildebrandslied*, which tells us that this poetic style was widespread.

Eddaic poems are, moreover, more like folk poems in the sense that they are not preserved as the works of single named poets, the way the skaldic poems are; and when they appear embedded in sagas and prose, they are often put into the mouths of divine figures or legendary heroes, whereas the skaldic poems usually come from human mouths. Iceland's single most precious manuscript from the Middle Ages contains nothing but a collection of these poems, the *Codex Regius of the Elder Edda* (written around 1270). Here they are presented systematically, beginning with mythological poems about the creation and the cosmic structure, and proceeding to more general stories about individual gods. Some of these are, in fact, very humorous. The second half contains heroic poems connected to the Nibelungen story, which is also well-known in Germany; many of these appear in Wagner's operas. Pictorial evidence also serves to show that this story was widespread over the Germanic cultural region.

These eddaic poems and Snorri's book on the myths are usually referred to as the *Eddas* — and they alone are enough to make Iceland's name stand out in the history of world literature. Iceland can also take pride in having managed to catch the old pagan heritage in writing without any significant influence of Christian ideas. This is due at least in part to the fact that, in Iceland, the art of poetry was venerated to such a degree that the clerical fathers would close their eyes to the non-Christian nature of much of its content.

The art of writing books, and using them to preserve and disseminate knowledge, was introduced to the pagan culture of north-western Europe through Christianity. The Church brought with it this new technique, and the whole approach to learning and religion that it entails. Even though runes were well-known in Scandinavia long before then, and were used for inscriptions and for incantations, they did not have the central function in society that writing and books had with Christianity. The passing on of the law and official life were all conducted orally, with the necessary witnesses to confirm everything that was said out loud. Traditional learning was also preserved orally, in stories and in poetry. Socially, this worked out perfectly well: people received education and training in law, genealogy, navigation, astronomy, ancient lore and legends, poetry, storytelling, and rhetoric — all without the aid of the written word.

By contrast, the *book* was used by the church as its medium for learning, and the whole of Christianity evolves around that symbol of the book — the *Bible* — which is placed on the altar. The sacred texts of the Bible managed to unite much larger population groups in the Middle Ages than had ever been united before, making such cultural phenomena as the crusades possible. This technique, this use of written texts for learning, came to Iceland after the introduction of

Christianity in the year 1000. It was first used for practical purposes within the church, particularly for clerical learning, utilizing, for example, translations of homilies and Saints' lives. This genre of writing in Iceland developed and later included works such as the lives of various Icelandic bishops, and even sagas about the kings of Norway (including, for example, the cruel missionary king Ólafur Haraldsson who, after his death, was gradually made into a saint). This Christian vein in Icelandic literature is very much on a par with what was going on in the rest of Europe, and thus is not of particular interest when discussing the medieval literary tradition in Iceland and its special place in literary history. The same can also be said for the European courtly literature that was translated into Icelandic in the 13th century, which inspired many to compose new sagas in the same courtly spirit. We must therefore be excused for not paying as much attention to these derivative parts of Iceland's literary heritage as to its more indigenous, and original, parts.

As the Church established itself within Icelandic society, it started to broaden its influence. Among the first secular materials to be put into writing were law texts, which were written down in the early 12th century, a little over a hundred years after the coming of Christianity. Thus was undermined the social status of the orally trained law speakers who no longer had the power to decide which was the correct law, but, instead, had to consult a written law book which was kept by the bishop!

The *Book of Icelanders*, *Íslendingabók*, written by Ari the Learned and dating from the third decade of the 12th century, is the second major achievement in the history of Icelandic letters. It is our oldest and most important source concerning the early settlement period in this country, as well as the Icelandic settlement in Greenland. Regrettably, it is told from a very clerical standpoint, focusing on the coming of Christianity and the history of the Church rather than on more secular, and perhaps more interesting, matters — for example, the Vínland voyages of which Ari obviously knew.

Later in the same century, another cleric, otherwise anonymous, wrote an original piece of work in which he tried to fit the Latin alphabet to Icelandic needs. In the process he analysed the language and its sound system, using the method of minimal pairs in the fashion of Chomsky and other modern linguists. It is fitting that his work has been called "The First Grammatical Treatise."

In the 12th century, secular chieftains also began to realise the power of the book as it was then that they started to compile the *Book of Settlements*, *Landnámabók*, which describes the original settlement around Iceland. This book, in a manner very typical of oral cultures, describes the first settlers in every firth and every valley as the present occupants wanted them remembered, and in the way that best suited their purposes, at that time. The versions now preserved, however, were rewritten in the 13th century and later, by people who added stories to the bare genealogies and lengthened and sometimes even tried to bend the family lines in order to include someone important or close to the heart of the scribe himself. This work is also remarkable for the fact that it describes the beginning of a whole new nation. It was certainly extremely influential in creating a shared sense of identity among the people who lived in Iceland, who could all trace back their origins in this single book.

As we near the end of the 12th century we see the dawning of an entirely new age in literary history: the Saga Age, or the golden age of Icelandic letters. The saga can be viewed as the forerunner of the modern novel; we can see its influence stretching from Sir Walter Scott and the development of the historical novel, through to Borges and the flourishing literature of Latin America. The first steps in that direction, however, were the writing of sagas about Norwegian kings. These gradually expanded and grew, and, at the height of their development, we again find Snorri Sturluson: his *Heimskringla,* generally thought to be the best collection of all, comprises sagas of kings ranging from the mythological past through to King Haraldur *hárfagri*, founder and king of the united Norwegian state at the time of the Icelandic settlement. This account of King Haraldur *hárfagri* is coloured, no doubt by the popular 13th century Icelandic view of the Viking settlers, their forefathers, as independent, literary individualists, for the most part, who had not been very happy with Haraldur's Union, and had therefore taken off for Iceland. The prototype for this type of Icelandic literary individualist is certainly Egill Skallagrímsson, whose saga was written in the first half of the 13th century, again possibly by Snorri Sturluson. *Egill's Saga*, which was written somewhere between 1230 and 1241, can be seen as the beginning of yet another new literary genre, the *Íslendingasögur,* or the *Sagas of the Icelanders.*

But Snorri was not alone in compiling sagas about kings. Others were doing the same, and constantly adding to what had already been written. This was done in a typically medieval fashion, and frequently short stories were added about Icelanders, often as poets, who had some connection with the different kings. The highest point of this additive process is to be found in an Icelandic manuscript from the end of the 14th century, *Flateyjarbók,* in which sagas about Norwegian kings are told more elaborately, and with more added material concerning Icelanders, than anywhere else, and which includes the only existing version of the *Greenlanders' Saga.*

With this activity, the Icelanders added to their list of unique literary productions: not only did they write down ancient oral poetry about the old Scandinavian gods and heroes, myths, and poems of praise about kings, but they also collected these into books, and told and retold their stories in readable and entertaining prose. They became the writers of royal history for Scandinavia: not only for Norway, but also for Denmark when sagas about the Danish kings were compiled (possibly by Ólafur *hvíti,* a nephew of Snorri), around the middle of the 13th century. However, these never became as popular as the sagas of the Norwegian kings. Around the year 1200, the earls of Orkney had a saga written about them, as did the Faroe Islanders and the Greenlanders. These sagas were about the settlement and Christianization periods in these countries, along the same literary lines as in the *Íslendingasögur* proper.

The Icelanders also wrote sagas about legendary Pan-Scandinavian heroes, set in the Viking Age: Ragnar *loðbrók* of Denmark, Örvar-Oddur, Hrólfur *kraki,* and many others, all of whom were probably widely known and celebrated in poetry throughout Scandinavia in former times, but are now only remembered in these Icelandic sagas. They are often regarded as a late literary development, even though many of the oldest saga manuscripts contain sagas of this type. It is safe to assume, however, that these characters, who appear in written sagas from the 13th century onwards, were also popular in oral stories with a continuous tradition going back to the Viking Age.

This massive production alone would be sufficient to make any small nation proud of itself, giving it courage to demand independence from foreign rule. But the ultimate source of Icelandic national pride is the group of works known as *Íslendingasögur,* the *Sagas of the Icelanders,* to which we are referring when we speak, simply, of the Icelandic sagas. These appeared on the literary scene in the first half of the 13th century, and continued to be a lively and creative literary genre for the next 200 years or so.

These 40 sagas, filling five volumes of almost 500 pages each in a recent English translation, tell of the Icelanders themselves during the first centuries of the Icelandic settlement period. These tales often begin in Norway, following the main characters across the Atlantic to Iceland where they face the difficulties and hardships of life in a new country, and continuing on through the coming of Christianity, which is generally regarded in a very positive light. In these sagas, the new Christianity often brings a peaceful solution to long-lasting blood feuds consisting in one act of revenge after another, and to internal family struggles in which the laws of duty bring family members into deadly opposition.

One thing that makes these sagas so fascinating is that many of them are exceptionally well-composed pieces of literature. They are often much more accessible to the modern reader than most of the commonly known examples of medieval literature from other countries, such as the *Chansons de Geste* from France, or the courtly romances. It is worthy of note that the world of the sagas is so coherent and often so realistic that many have been tempted to regard them as descriptions of real life, even though they are all supposed to have taken place 200 or 300 years before they were written. From one saga to another, genealogies correspond, and the same chieftains appear; in unrelated sagas, the same laws and customs show up — all giving the impression that what is being described is a real society which it is possible to reconstruct, with the sagas as field reports. Characters from the sagas are not merely literary prototypes, as is often the case in heroic literature, but are more like flesh-and-blood people whom we seem to know as well as our old schoolmates. Many are felt as family friends in today's Icelandic homes, and are quoted for their wit and their expressions of deep feelings of sorrow and joy.

At the same time as the Icelanders were writing down all this ancient material, they were also focusing on their own contemporary history, writing yet another chronicle unique by any standards: the so-called *Sturlunga-saga*. This is actually a compilation of a number of sagas which centre on internal family feuds in the 12th and 13th centuries. These feuds, which led up to several battles in the mid-13th century, were not finally resolved until the Icelanders swore allegiance to the Norwegian king, around 1262.

Given how massive this literary outpouring was in the Middle Ages, we are bound to ask: is it really true that the Icelanders were so unique in these matters? Did not their Scandinavian contemporaries, their relations in fact, also know how to write? And if the Icelanders really were so original, what explanation is there that might throw some light on the cause of all this?

It seems quite clear that, from the very beginning, Icelandic culture, especially its literary culture, was radically different from that of the Norwegians. As we have seen, Icelanders were the only Nordic nation in the Middle Ages who wrote literature in the vernacular, and almost all the identifiable court poets in Scandinavia came from Iceland. Several theories have been proposed to account for this. The Scandinavian chroniclers, Theodoricus and Saxo Grammaticus who wrote in Latin around 1200, were already aware of the special position of the Icelanders in the oral tradition of verbal art, referring to them as the preservers of ancient lore.[1]

Some modern scholars, mostly Scandinavians, have argued that the Icelanders were, in fact, by no means unique. Rather, the rise of the Icelandic literary tradition can be explained by the special circumstances attending the settlement of this Arctic community, and by the

influence of continental works that are thought to have inspired the
12th- and 13th-century development of the Icelandic sagas. These
sagas are often regarded as a natural development of the earlier sagas
about Norwegian kings, and these, in turn, are seen as an offshoot of
still earlier hagiographic works. It has been claimed, however, that
such a development is far from self-evident, and that it is not to the
Latin learning of the time that we should turn, seeking the ultimate
inspiration for these literary works. Instead, it can be found in the
oral tradition in Iceland, with its origins in the cultural mix that
resulted from the convergence of settlers from Norway and the
British Isles forming a common community several centuries earlier.
In other words, they suggest that the answer is to be found in the
Gaelic contribution to Icelandic culture, as the Irish and the Scots had
a much more developed standard of the literary arts than the Scandinavians at that time.

In the present work, this much discussed hypothesis will be mooted
once again: that Icelandic literature was influenced by the Gaelic
world where oral literature was highly developed and written prose
sagas were produced in the vernacular. Ireland and Iceland are the
only countries in north-western Europe where sagas of this kind were
written down, and this has caused many scholars to assume that there
must be some connection between the two. In fact, I know of no
scholar dealing with the problem who has totally rejected all Gaelic
influence in Iceland. The difficulty arises when the importance of
that influence on Icelandic culture has to be assessed.

In the first four chapters, I consider possible routes for Gaelic cultural influence to have reached Iceland: 1) via Norsemen who came
from Ireland and Scotland in the 9th and 10th centuries, where they
had come into contact with native Gaelic culture (as can be seen from
borrowed Irish vocabulary, especially place names, military alliances,
mutual fosterages, the "Foreign Irish," and the recent Viking excavations in Dublin); 2) via cultural contacts in the Orkneys, where the
Norsemen were in close contact with the Gaelic inhabitants; and 3)
with people of Gaelic extraction who settled in Iceland, either as free
settlers, as wives of Norsemen, or as slaves. Slaves are often referred

to in Icelandic sources, but rarely receive much attention. For Gaelic influence to have had a profound effect on Icelandic culture, it is argued here that the last mentioned route is the most likely. Even though the first two suggested routes may have had some influence, they were likely to have had similar effects in Norway and can not, therefore, account for the apparent literary uniqueness of Iceland.

Gaelic influence in Iceland is also found in a number of old borrowed words and personal names. These include words such as brekán=breacan/breccán, gjalt=geilt, kapall= capall, and tarfur=tarb, and names such as Dufgus=Dubgus, Njáll=Niáll, Kormákur=Cormac, and (Myr-) Kjartan= Muircheartach. There are several possible factors which may account for the fact that these are not more numerous, including that 1) the Gaels did not contribute any new work skills or crafts, carrying their own vocabulary, into the mainly Norse controlled society; 2) their work was supervised by Norsemen; 3) the slaves were often renamed with Norse names; and 4) the language of the slaves was probably not widely spoken by their masters.

The low social status of most of the Gaels in Iceland may also explain why Gaelic named heroes do not appear in Icelandic works, even though numerous instances have been traced of Gaelic influenced motifs and ideas in the Icelandic literary corpus. This influence is mainly found in the works most closely related to the oldest literary tradition in Iceland, namely the *Fornaldarsögur* (the *Legendary Sagas*) and the mythological material, as discussed in chapters 5 and 6. It would appear likely that the *Fornaldarsögur*, which are set in the Viking Age and describe the adventures of Scandinavians of that time, were founded on older Scandinavian poetic lore, which was recast as oral prose narrative in Iceland. The framework for the mythological tales, as we know them from Snorri's *Prose-Edda* and the eddaic poems, is without doubt Scandinavian. But within that frame, stories could be added and changed, thus allowing Gaelic motifs to penetrate Scandinavian mythology and be attached to the Norse gods. The literary genres that developed in Iceland, such as the *Kings' Sagas* and the *Sagas of the Icelanders*, show fewer traces of Gaelic influence, though some such leavening may be found in particular *in Sagas* which come from areas where Gaels are known to have been prominent. This is discussed at length in chapter 7. Examples can be drawn from *Laxdœla saga*, which begins with the settlement in Iceland of the widow of a Viking king in Dublin, and *Kjalnesinga saga,* in which several settlers come from the British Isles.

Irish material is also to be found when the scene moves to the Gaelic world, such as in the Icelandic accounts of *Brjánsbardagi* (the *Battle of Clontarf*), in *Njáls saga,* and in *Þorsteins saga Síðu-Hallssonar.*

Skaldic poetry fits well into this picture, as presented in the final chapter of this book. This poetry was mainly practised by Icelanders, and most poets of any repute came from areas where Gaels were known to have been among the first settlers. There is evidence to suggest that the art of skaldic poetry was acquired through special training, though this seems, in Iceland, to have taken place within certain families rather than at professional schools, as was the practice in Ireland. Additionally, skaldic metres differ considerably from older Germanic and Scandinavian metres, but show similarities to those found in Old Irish poetry. The comparison of these, however, has proven notoriously complicated as can be seen from Stephen N. Tranter's work from 1997: *Clavis Metrica: Háttatal, Háttalykill and the Irish Metrical Tracts.*

It is not my intention to analyse all of these literary genres and motifs in order to find out whether a connection, in each separate case, can be regarded as proved. Since other scholars in recent decades have been concerned mainly with individual motifs, I deemed it more useful to look at the nature of the numerous parallels between different categories of Old Icelandic literature and Gaelic literature, Old Irish in particular, parallels already pointed out by others. By so doing, I hope not only to provide a comprehensive bibliography of the subject, but also to assess what these parallels can tell us about the importance of Gaelic influence in the

Icelandic literary tradition. In the process, the nature of what is known and what may yet be discovered should become clear — or rather, perhaps, how little indeed can be known with any certainty!

1 See Historia Danica, pp. 7–8: "Nec Tylensium industria silentio obliteranda; qui cum ob nativam soli sterilatatem luxuriae nutrimentis carentes officia continuae sobrietatis exerceant omniaque vitae momenta ad excolendam alienorum operum notitiam conferre soleant, inopiam ingenio pensant. Cunctarum quippe nationum res gestas cognosse memoriaeque mandare voluptatis loco reputant, non minoris gloriae judicantes alieneas virtutes disserere, quam proprias exhibere. Quorum thesauros historicarum rerum pignoribus refertos curiosius consulens, haud parvam praesentis operis partem ex eorum relationis imitatione contexui, nec arbitros habere contempsi, quos tanta vetustatis peritia callere cognovi." ("The diligence of the men of Iceland must not be shrouded in silence; since the barrenness of their native soil offers no means of self-indulgence, they pursue a steady routine of temperance and devote all their time to improving our knowledge of others' deeds, compensating for poverty by their intelligence. They regard it a real pleasure to discover and commemorate the achievements of every nation; in their judgement it is as elevating to discourse on the prowess of others as to display their own. Thus I have scrutinised their store of historical treasures and composed a considerable part of this present work by copying their narratives, not scorning, where I recognized such skill in ancient lore, to take these men as witnesses" — Transl. by P. Fisher (1979) 5). And Theodoricus says about the Icelanders when talking about old knowledge: "hæc in suis antiquis carminibus percelebrata recolunt" ("They remember these often mentioned things in their old poems"). Quotation from G. Storm (1880) 3. See also Bjarni Guðnason (1977). He argues that Theodoricus had access to twelfth century Icelandic books even though he used oral informants as well.

Chapter I

VIKING CONTACTS WITH THE IRISH IN THE BRITISH ISLES BEFORE 1014

1.1. Pre-Viking Contacts

Pre-Viking contacts in the British Isles between Scandinavia and the Gaelic world have been claimed on the evidence of archaeological finds,[1] Scandinavian place-names in the Northern Isles (Shetland and the Orkneys) which suggest a pre-Viking settlement there,[2] and Irish chronicles which mention a raiding fleet on Tory Island, north-west of Donegal, in 612 (616/617) and a raid on Eigg in the southern Hebrides in 617.[3]

---

1 A. Bugge (1905) 307ff and (1912) 119-20; H. Shetelig (1940) 7-8, who drew attention to a certain kind of strike-a-light common in Norwegian graves from the 5th and 6th centuries but unheard of in younger graves and elsewhere in Europe except on the Scottish Isles and NE-Ireland. These findings point very strongly to contacts long before A.D. 800. Shetelig's dating, however, is no longer regarded as certain so this evidence must be treated carefully (P. Wallace - personal communication).

2 J. Jakobsen (1901) 68-69, 104-110, 164-69, who argued that place-names on the Shetlands, ending in "-vin" and "-heimr" must have been formed before 800 because they were not used to form new place-names in Norway so late, and suggested a Norse colonization of the islands about 700. A. Bugge (1905) 312ff, used Jakobsen's conclusions and suggested a Norse settlement "endnu tidligere" (317) ("much earlier") and C.J.S. Marstrander (1915) 1-4, wanted to put it as far back as the 6th century.

3 *Annals of the Kingdom of Ireland by the Four Masters* (AFM) 612; *Annals of Ulster* (AU) 616; A.O. Anderson (1922) 142-43. H. Zimmer (1891) 308ff, was the first to suggest that this fleet and the raiders might have been Scandinavian. He was later supported by A. Bugge (1905) 11-12, (1912) 119-20 and C.J.S. Marstrander (1915) 1-4 who both thought that this fleet came from Norse settlements in the Northern Isles. As late as 1957, A. Sommerfelt, 5, was

The artefacts, however, which have been found in Scandinavia and have been taken to point to early contacts, are few in number and may even be explained by later influence.[4] Norse Settlement in the Northern Isles is now seen as commencing about A.D. 800[5] and the raiding fleet in 612 (616/617) need not have been Scandinavian[6] but might have been of Pictish origin.[7]

still inclined to think of these raiders as Scandinavian and in 1958 he added that the Old-Norse name for the Picts, "péttar/péttir", must have been formed before 700, using linguistic evidence to support his claim, thus pointing to earlier contacts with Scotland than 800.

4 Finnur Jónsson (1921) 13ff, who argued against all these contacts and said: "Jeg føler mig overbevist om, at hele Bugges antagelse, der knyttes til disse billedstene, svæver fuldstændig i luften." (15-16) ("I am entirely convinced that the ideas Bugge derives from these picture-stones, hang completely in the air.")
5 Finnur Jónsson (1921) 12; A.W. Brøgger (1929) 5, where he suggested a bracket of 780-850, and later in 1930 where he says that "... landnåmstiden [i.e. the Norse settlement of the islands], stort sett tilhører tiden 800-860..." (238) ("The Age of Settlement is basically between 800 and 860.") but allows for some immigration already in the 8th century. Also F.T. Wainwright (1962) 126, and more recently Small (1976) 29, who both agree on a date about the year 800. Small, referring to Sommerfelt (1958) allows for "sporadic contacts [...] between Scotland and Norway before A.D. 800." (29) We may also note that A.A.M. Duncan (1975) 83, suggested that the Northern Isles were used as staging posts by Scandinavian seafarers before they settled down on the islands. He draws on the evidence of names in "-ey", "-nes", and "-fjall" on the islands where most inland topographical names are Gaelic—which suggests that these features in the landscape were used for navigation by the Norsemen and thus originally named from the sea.
6 Finnur Jónsson (1921) 9ff, and F.T. Wainwright (1962) who says: "His [Zimmer's] suggestion, which has confused several subsequent writers, is no more than an unsupported speculation." (130)
7 Finnur Jónsson (1921) 10. According to Beda I. 12 (B. Colgrave and R.A.B. Mynors (1969) 42-43), the Picts were known to raid from the sea. H. Zimmer (1891) had argued against the Pictish origin, saying that "darüber wäre, bei der genauen Bekanntschaft der Nordiren mit den Pikten, eine Notiz uns erhalten: mit einer solchen That hätte man sie in den Annalen gebrandmarkt."(311) ("Due to the close contacts between the Northern Irish and the Picts, that would have been mentioned: with such a deed one would have branded them [i.e. the Picts] in the annals.")

1.2. *Ninth and Tenth Century Contacts*

It is not until the Viking raids start in full force in the 9th century that any permanent link between the Gaelic and Scandinavian peoples can be established. The Northern Isles were probably the first to be settled by Norwegians in search for land where they soon became the ruling class in what seems to have been a peaceful procedure.[8]

By the middle of the 9th century the Vikings had built fortifications, later to develop into towns, in various parts of Ireland. All through the 9th century there are records of Viking raids against the Irish as well as of the Vikings making alliances with the Irish who were fighting among themselves before and after the arrival of the Vikings in Ireland.[9] In recent decades, scholars reevaluating the role of the Vikings in Ireland have pointed out that they were not so much invading the country as an external military force but rather came as a motley migrant group, consisting of merchants, pirates and settlers who were most likely looked upon as just another tribe in Ireland.[10]

8 A.Fenton (1978) 12-17.

9 The main sources for Viking activities in Ireland are the Irish annals and a 12th century work, *Cogadh Gaedhel re Gallaibh (The War of the Gaedhil with the Gaill)*. A discussion of the historical value of these sources can be found in P. Sawyer (1962) 25-28 and K. Hughes (1972) 144-48 and 288-97. For a similar discussion, see also D. Ó Corráin (1974). The annals, especially the *Annals of Ulster*, even though written from a monastic point of view, appear to give a fairly reliable picture of Viking activities since they record raids by the Irish as well as those of the Vikings (K. Hughes (1969) 25). *The War of the Gaedhil with the Gaill*, on the other hand must be treated more carefully (K. Hughes (1969) 24). For a good summary of the history of the Vikings in Ireland, see D. Ó Corráin (1972). For more detailed accounts with special reference to Irish-Norse relations in Ireland, see A. Bugge (1900); A. Walsh (1922) and J.I. Young (1950). Also C. Haliday (1881).

10 P. Sawyer (1962) and (1970); A.T. Lucas (1966) and (1967). As a result of this change in attitude towards the Vikings, i.e. in not merely regarding them

Towards the end of the 9th century the Norse of Dublin faced internal struggles which resulted in their expulsion from Dublin in 902. From 914 onwards, Viking attacks in Ireland resumed. Dublin was the centre for their activities once again but instead of being a separate group they became more and more integrated into the Irish political scene. This is exemplified in their part in the Battle of Clontarf (1014) which has been interpreted traditionally as an Irish victory over the foreign invaders, marking the end of Norse reign in Dublin. Now it seems that "... Clontarf was part of the internal struggle for sovereignty and was essentially the revolt of the Leinstermen against the dominance of Brian, a revolt in which their Norse allies played an important but secondary role."[11]

But what can be said about the nature of Norse-Irish relationships in terms of cultural excahange? To what extent did the Vikings become acquainted with Irish culture and the Irish with that of the Vikings?

The Vikings arrived as pagans but became Christian during their stay in Ireland. On the evidence of references to the Norsemen in the annals it has been suggested that the Norse who left Dublin in 902, and before, had accepted Christianity. Up to 850/860 the Norsemen are most commonly referred to in the *Annals of Ulster* as "geinte" (gentiles, heathens) but after that, they are normally called "foreigners" (*Gaill*) or "Norsemen" (*Nordmanni*). When pagan Vikings reappear in Ireland

---

as raiders, some scholars have tended to neglect their raiding activities. C.P. Wormald (1982) has drawn attention to this, saying "... that though the Vikings may not have been mad, they were probably bad, and certainly dangerous to know." (148). Sawyer (1982) himself has now also reassessed their status as raiders of the Western world.

11 D.Ó Corráin (1972) 130. See also J. Ryan (1938) and A.J. Goedheer (1938). Even as early as the end of the 9th century it has been said that: "The Vikings had in fact become little more than an element in the complex of Irish politics, and even as early as 850 some native rulers had formed alliances with them." (P. Sawyer (1982) 85).

in the early 10th century the annals again refer to them as
heathens (mainly from 912-922).[12]
Place-name evidence in England, where some of the emigrants from Dublin upto 902 went, suggests that they knew some

12 D.Ó Corráin (1972) 96. It is debatable how much emphasis can be laid
on the different terms used to describe the Vikings. Already from 826, onwards, the AU occasionally refer to them as foreigners even though the word
for "heathens" is used 3 or 4 times as often. It is significant as well that when the
Vikings are driven out of Dublin in 902, the AU (901) say that "The heathens
were driven from Ireland, i.e. from the fortress of Áth Cliath" ("Indarba
ngennti a hEre, .í. longport Atha Cliath") which suggests that their faith may
have been somewhat dubious. The last references to them as "heathens" before
that are under 867 and 876. In 867, in fact, it seems that the annalist is using the
terms for "foreigners" and "heathens" as synonyms: "Aed son of Niall won a
battle at Cell Ua nDaigri against the Uí Néill of Brega, and the Laigin, and a
large force of the foreigners, i.e. three hundred or more; and Flann son of
Conaing, king of all Brega and Diarmait son of Etarscéle, king of Loch Gabor,
fell therein; and in this battle very many of the heathens were slaughtered"
("Bellum re nAedh m. Neill oc Cill Oa nDaighri for Ou Neill Breg 1 for
Laighniu 1 for sluagh mor di Ghallaibh, .i. tri cét uel eo amplius, in quo
ceciderunt Flann m. Conaing rig Bregh n-utile, 1 Diarmit m. Etersceili, ri Locha
Gabhor;1 in isto bello plurimi gentilium trucidati sunt;"). As late as under 942
(the last reference to "heathens" in the AU) a similar tendency may be
observed: "Muirchertach son of Niall [...] was killed by the heathens, [...] Ard
Macha was plundered by the same foreigners on the following day" ("Muirchertach m. Neill, [...] do marbad do ghentibh [...] Ard Macha do arcain [...] o na
Gallaib cetnaib.") In spite of these precautions in interpreting the evidence it
remains clear that on the whole there is a significant difference between
different periods as to whether the Vikings are described as "foreigners" or
"heathens". Fresh invaders are much more likely to be called heathens whereas
residents of settled communities are more commonly looked upon as foreigners. L.J. Vogt (1896) 327; A. Walsh (1922) 48; J.I. Young (1950) 24; D.Ó
Corráin (1972) 96, have all argued that an entry for 872 in the B-text of the
AU, recording the death of Ívar, king of the Norse in Dublin, should be
interpreted as a sign of his conversion to Christianity. It reads: "... in Christo
quievit" ("... he rested in Christ"). The problem however is that the B-text is a
copy of the so-called A-text which is supposed to be closer to the original (S.
Mac Airt and G. Mac Niocaill (1983) viii). The A-text has "... vitam finiuit" so
the reference to Christ must be a later addition by a scribe and the argument
therefore of no value (A and B are used in W.M. Hennessy and B. Mac Carthy's
edition but S. Mac Airt and G. Mac Niocaill use H and R respectively).

19

Irish.[13] Some of the Norwegian settlers in Iceland were probably among those who left Dublin during this period,[14] and may have brought with them knowledge of Christianity. In Iceland we know of Auðr djúpúðga, a Christian settler in the west. She is said to have been the wife of Ólafr hvíti, king of Dublin, and left Dublin after his death, coming to Iceland via the Hebrides. Auðr is not mentioned in Irish sources but can be regarded as an example of an emigrant from Dublin in the late 9th century, bringing Christianity to Iceland.

The Vikings who arrived in Dublin in the 10th century settled in a different place from that inhabited by their 9th century predecessors.[15] Throughout the 10th century, however, they were gradually Christianized and in 1014 Dublin is described as a fully Christian city.[16]

Even though the Norse seem to have become an integral part of Irish society in the beginning of the 11th century they preserved their language to some extent until the 13th and some kind of ethnical identity even as late as the 14th.[17]

From the middle of the 9th century onwards, we hear of the Norse marrying Irish women and as a result of such marriages

13 Ekwall (1924) 34; A.H. Smith (1928) xxi-xxii, xxvi-xxix, and W.G. Collingwood (1927).

14 D. Ó Corráin (1972) 95-96; J.I. Young (1950) 28; P.H. Sawyer (1970). Sawyer (88-89) suggests that the reappearance of Vikings in Ireland in the 10th century may be explained by the idea that by then new areas like Iceland no longer offered as good land for settlement as before, which in turn directed the Norsemen to Ireland again.

15 The exact location of the 9th century settlement is unknown but it has been suggested that it was somewhere near the Kilmainham/Islandsbridge area in Dublin, whereas the 10th century settlement was further down the Liffey where it has now been excavated. J. Graham-Campbell (1976) 40; P. Wallace (1982) 138-48; H. Murray (1983) 2. See also for a general survey of the excavation: P. Wallace (1985).

16 After 922 the AU very rarely refer to the Norsemen as "heathens". Ólafr Kvaran, king of Dublin 953-81 was baptized in England and ended his life on a pilgrimage to Iona in 981 (see L.J. Vogt (1896) 328ff; A. Bugge (1900) 289-92; J.I. Young (1950) 28-29).

17 A. Bugge (1900) 306-25.

we hear of the *Gall-Ghaedhil* ("foreign Irish") who were probably of mixed parentage and most likely bilingual, at least to some extent.[18] In the same century, mutual fosterage was known,[19] the Norse used Irish names,[20] and military alliances were frequent.[21] It may be suggested that the Norse could understand and enjoy Irish literary entertainment in the 10th century. In a poem by chief poet Cinaed ua hArtacáin[22] it says that the poem is composed for Amlaib of Ath Cliath (most likely Ólafr Kvaran, king of Dublin) and that the poet was rewarded for it.[23]

The evidence from the excavations of the Viking town itself is irrelevant in an examination of the 9th century Norse since only the 10th century settlement has been discovered.[24] The only thing that has been found from the 9th century is a cemetery with graves of both men and women along with objects, which all points to a settled community rather than to one of transient warriors.[25] Evidence from the 10th century enables us to conclude that the inhabitants of Dublin seem to have carried out peaceful trading with their Irish neighbours. It also seems that the Dublin settlers have lost some of their Scandinavian

18 J.C.H.R. Steenstrup (1878) 126-29; A. Bugge (1900) 280-82; C.J.S. Marstrander (1915) 4-11; A. Walsh (1922) 14-17; J.I. Young (1950) 19, 24.

19 J.I. Young (1950) 18.

20 A. Bugge (1900) 284-5 for 9th and pp. 285-8 for 10th century. See also W. Faraday (1900) 18-20.

21 J.I. Young (1950) 22-3 for 9th and p. 26 for 10th century. Lucas (1966) 65-67.

22 AU 974 (not 874 as misprinted in A.T. Lucas (1966) 67): "Cinaed ua hArtacáin, [...] chief poet of Ireland, rested" ("Cinaed H. Artugan, [...] primecess E*renn*, quieuit.").

23 E.Gwynn (1903) 52-53, 80, 82: "Amlaib Átha Cliath cétaig // rogab rígi i mBeind Étair; // tallus lúag mo dúane de, // ech d'echaib ána Aichle." ("Amlaib of Ath Cliath the hundred-strong, // who gained the kingship in Bend Etair; // I bore off from him as price of my song // a horse of the horses of Achall.") 52-53.

24 See H. Murray (1983) 1-2; P.F. Wallace (1982).

25 G. Coffey and E.C.R. Armstrong (1910).

identity at this stage, which is understandable if it is assumed that they had not come directly from Scandinavia but from Britain where they had come under influence of the Anglo-Saxons.[26] It appears that the Norse did not learn advanced woodworking techniques, already well established among the native Irish, until the 11th century[27] and this fact weakens the theory of intimate cultural relationship. The Norse conservatism with regard to woodwork might be explained by the suggestion that most of the excavated houses seem to have been owner-built without any carpenters' assistance.[28]

Norse influence apparently affected Irish society already in the 9th century. Irish weapons from the second half of that century show strong Viking influence[29] and it has been suggested that these were not imitations made by the Irish since the

... phenomenon can be more adequately explained by the existence of a close relationship, commercial and social, between the Norse communities and the neighbouring Irish, which entailed a country-wide system of barter by Norse merchants and, perhaps, the free interchange of technical skills between craftsmen on both sides.[30]

In the early 10th century, Irish fleets appear, on a larger scale than before, probably due to Viking influence,[31] which is also suggested by Norse loanwords in Irish, mainly in the fields of warfare, seafaring and commerce.[32]

26 P.F. Wallace (1982).

27 P.F. Wallace (1982*) 296.

28 H. Murray (1983) 85-86. This, however, need not necessarily be correct (P. Wallace — personal communication).

29 E. Rynne (1966) and J.P. Mallory (1982).

30 A.T. Lucas (1966) 73.

31 A. Walsh (1922) 35-9. As in the case of the weapons, Lucas (1966) 71, suggests that the Irish employed Norsemen for shipbuilding.

32 See esp. C.J.S. Marstrander (1915), but also W.A. Craigie (1894); A. Bugge (1912*); K. Meyer (1918); A. Walsh (1922) 40-43; A. Sommerfelt (1962).

Surprisingly enough, Vikings do not appear much in the Irish literature of the time. The explanation for this might be that its "... form and content were already too well established and its antiquity too well respected"[33] to allow any intrusion. This does not, of course, mean that stories about the Vikings could not have entered local oral tradition and become part of Irish folklore.[34]

It remains more difficult to assess to what extent the Norse in Dublin were influenced by the Irish. No Norse texts from the area have survived and Irish loanwords in Old Icelandic literature are few. But it may also be that even though Irish words were frequent in everyday speech among the Norse in Dublin, they are likely to have fallen out of use in Iceland just like Gaelic names and Christianity.[35]

The evidence of Norse-Irish contacts as early as the 9th century does nevertheless suggest that it was possible for the Norse in Dublin to enjoy and acquire some knowledge of Irish oral literature before some of them left the city towards the end of the 9th century. Settlers in Iceland, both former residents of Dublin or other Scandinavian colonies in Ireland, and those who had only visited that part of the world on their travels, could, therefore, have brought Irish stories with them to Iceland. It is a debatable point, however, whether such second-hand knowledge of storytelling and deep-rooted literary tradition was enough to build up a culture in Iceland in total contrast to the original Norwegian one. As was mentioned above and will be discussed again, the Christian settlers who came from the Gaelic world, some of whom bore Gaelic names, seem to have relinquished their newly acquired customs, and their descendants soon adopted both pagan beliefs and Norse names.[36]

33 P. Mac Cana (1962) 97. See for an example of a Germanic motif probably finding its way into Irish tradition: Bo Almqvist (1965).
34 R.T. Christiansen (1930).
35 A. Bugge (1900) 299.
36 The lack of loanwords and Gaelic names in Iceland was used by W.A.

23

If the radical difference between Iceland and Norway as reflected in Old-Icelandic literature, is to be explained by Gaelic influence, it must be assumed that a substantial immigration of Gaels into Iceland took place. If any such evidence can be found, it remains to be explained why Gaelic loanwords and names are not more common than they are.

Craigie (1894), (1897) and (1897*); and W. Faraday (1900) who both argued that the Norse in Ireland knew but little of the Irish. They also mentioned that the Irish sources reflect little knowledge of the Norse and references in the Icelandic Sagas to people going to Ireland must be looked upon as exceptional rather than customary. Finnur Jónsson (1921) thoroughly scrutinizing the written evidence of early Christianity, Gaelic names and loanwords in Iceland, gives his full support to Craigie's ideas (44, 64).

Chapter II

THE GAELS IN ICELAND

2.1. Papar

Íslendingabók, written about 1130 by Ari fróði, mentions that before the Norwegians settled in Iceland, from 870 onwards, some Irish hermits, known as *papar*, used to live on the island but left soon after their peace was disturbed by the Norwegians, leaving behind them books, bells and bagles.[1] The validity of Ari's statement has been much discussed and very little has been found in Iceland which points to settlement much earlier than 870. In Vestmannaeyjar, excavations carried out in the seventies revealed a settlement earlier than 870, but what was found there points to a Norse settlement rather than to that of Irish hermits.[2] Excavations on sites where place-names refer to *papar*, such as Papey, have not produced any evidence either. A few bells, however, have been found in 10th century graves but they tell us little about Irish hermits.[3] Ari does not therefore get much support from archaeology. The Irish monk, Dicuil, however, writing about 825, refers to clerics who had lived on an island called Thule — most likely Iceland — about 790.[4] In

---

1 "Þá váru hér menn kristnir, þeir es Norðmenn kalla papa, en þeir fóru síðan á braut, af því at þeir vildu eigi vesa hér við heiðna menn, ok létu eptir bœkur írskar ok bjǫllur og bagla; af því mátti skilja, at þeir váru menn írskir." *Íslendingabók*, 5. *Landnámabók*, 31-32, has a similar passage which is probably derived from *Íslendingabók*.

2 Margrét Hermannsdóttir (1982).

3 Kristján Eldjárn (1966).

4 See J.J. Tierney (1967) VII, 11, p. 74-5: "It is now thirty years since clerics, who lived on the island [i.e. Thule] from the first of February to the first of August, told me that not only at the summer solstice, but in the days round about it, the sun setting in the evening hides itself as though behind a small hill

25

fact there is no great reason to doubt that these stories have some basis in reality. The combined evidence of the literary sources and the place-names carries much weight.[5] But even though we accept it as a fact that Irish hermits lived in Iceland before 870 we are no closer to a source for Irish influence on Icelandic culture. Whether they left or stayed when the Norwegians arrived, matters little. Monastic communities cannot survive anywhere for more than one generation unless new blood is brought in from external sources, since hermits do not, of course, reproduce among themselves.

When Iceland was fully inhabited by Norwegians there was no reason for Irish hermits to go there since they could no longer live in solitude there. No Irish hermits are therefore likely to have come to Iceland after 870.

Whatever influence these monastic settlements might have exercised on their surrounding hostile and pagan communities, the *papar* could not remain for long in Iceland and must be excluded as major contributors to Icelandic culture. We must seek other explanations.

2.2. Gaelic Settlers

Gaelic people are found in Iceland as independent settlers, as wives of Norwegian settlers and as slaves. Of these three

in such a way that there was no darkness in that very small space of time, and a man could do whatever he wished as though the sun were there, even remove lice from his shirt, and if they had been on a mountain-top perhaps the sun would never have been hidden from them." ("Trigesimus nunc annus est a quo nuntiauerunt mihi clerici qui a kalendis Febroarii usque kalendas Augusti in illa insula manserunt quod non solum in aestiuo solstitio sed in diebus circa illud in uespertina hora occidens sol abscondit se quasi trans paruulum tumulum, ita ut nihil tenebrarum in minimo spatio ipso fiat, sed quicquid homo operari uoluerit uel peduculos de camisia abstrahere tamquam in presentia solis potest. Et si in altitudine montium eius fuissent, forsitan numquam sol absconderetur ab illis.")
5 Einar Ólafur Sveinsson (1945); Björn Sigfússon (1958); Hermann Pálsson (1965); Guðrún Sveinbjarnardóttir (1972). See also Halldór Laxness (1965).

categories, *Landnámabók* is most likely to name the independent settlers. Wives of Gaelic extraction are rarely mentioned by name and slaves, if referred to at all, usually appear as an anonymous group; sometimes Norse names have been given to them by their masters.[6]

TABLE I[7]

Distribution of place-names and archaeological material, possibly reflecting early Gaelic influence.

Sýslur	'Celtic' placen.	Kirkju- ból	Kross farms	pagan graves	Corbelled houses
Rangárv.s.	10	0	6	21	45
Vestm.eyjar	1	0	1	0	3*
Árnessýsla	12	0	4	11	24*
Gullb.Kjós.	6	1	1	2	36
Borgf.Mýr.	16	3	5	3	7
Snæf.Hnapp.	18	0	4	2	216*
Dalasýsla	19	0	2	2	7
Barðastr.s.	17	5	4	4	22*
Ísafj.s.	5	10	1	2	21
Strandas.	0	2	1	0	2
Húnavatnss.	10	0	3	12	2
Skagafj.	7	0	3	11	0
Eyjafj.	2	0	3	24	3
S.-Þing.	3	0	3	14	3
N.-Þing.	1	0	3	3	0
N.-Múlas.	1	0	3	14	28
S.-Múlas.	4	4	1	4	17
A.-Skaftaf.	5	0	2	2	46
V.-Skaftaf.	0	1	1	4	32

6 W.A. Craigie (1897*); A. Bugge (1905) 359ff; Einar Ólafur Sveinsson (1962) 18ff.

7 This table is taken from Þorvaldur Friðriksson (1982) 94. The figures marked with* refer mainly to fishermen's huts, the number of which is uncertain.

Of all the names in *Landnámabók,* only about 2% can be described as Gaelic[8] and most of these no longer survive in Iceland. It is interesting to note, however, that the Gaelic settlers mentioned in *Landnámabók* seem mainly to be confined to certain areas in the western, south-western, southern and south-eastern parts of the country. This corresponds to the distribution of place-names containing Gaelic elements (see Table I for this and the following), which are most common in the West and South.[9] Further it may be noted that place-names connected with Christianity and likely to be earlier than the year 1000[10] are more frequent in these areas than elsewhere, and corbelled houses, believed to reflect Gaelic influence, are also mainly found there.[11] It is also worth noting that pagan burials are mostly found outside these areas.[12]

It is clear from the table that the four factors pointing to Gaelic influence are all to be found in the western, south-western and southern parts of Iceland. Regarding the amount of pagan burials in the south, it must be pointed out that they seem most common east of Rangá and north of Markarfljót whereas the Gaelic elements are mainly outside that district.[13] The

8 W.A. Craigie (1897) 441.

9 Hermann Pálsson (1952), (1953). Also A. Bugge (1905) 359ff and Finnur Jónsson (1921) 46-51. I am indepted to Þorvaldur Friðriksson (1982) 85-96, who has gathered the information on this distribution and set it up on maps.

10 According to an unpublished work by Sigríður Erlendsdóttir and referred to in Þorvaldur Friðriksson (1982) 88.

11 Þorvaldur Friðriksson (1982) 93-96.

12 Kristján Eldjárn (1956) 196-99, who suggested that the confinement of pagan burials to the central North and certain areas in the South and East should be explained by different methods of roadwork in these areas than elsewhere. The roadwork activity is then supposed to have revealed these graves. As Þorvaldur Friðriksson (1982) 91, has shown, this explanation is rather unlikely since roads have been built all over the country. He points out that 'Celtic'-Christian influence seems to be stronger where pagan burials have not been found which might suggest that 'Celtic' influence was stronger in these areas than *Landnámabók* allows us to conclude.

13 Þorvaldur Friðriksson (1982), 90, 92.

28

common occurrence of corbelled houses in the South-East
might be connected with the fact that most *papar* place-names
are in this area.

Still another point to be added is that most poets' families in
the first centuries of colonization in Iceland come from the
areas where, according to the above mentioned evidence,
Gaelic influence seems to have been strongest.[14]
Even though this evidence does little more than confirm what
Landnámabók says about a certain percentage of the settlers
being Gaelic,[15] we know for certain that *Landnámabók* by no
means mentions all the people who came to Iceland. It concen-
trates on independent settlers and since there is no doubt that
the ruling class in Iceland was of Norse origin it is not surprising
that most of these are from Norway. The lower classes, servants, slaves etc., who tend to be more numerous in any society
than the upper classes, are hardly dealt with. It is therefore
highly questionable whether we are entitled to look in *Landnámabók* for information on place of origin of the population *in
toto*.

It has been estimated that the first settlers in Iceland were
about 20.000 persons out of which *Landnámabók* mentions
about 5%.[16] The absurdity of drawing on *Landnáma* in estimating the proportion of Gaelic people in Iceland, has been
conveniently summarised by Jón Steffensen[17] who said:

Til að fá sennilega útkomu verður [...] að áætla eitthvert skynsamlegt hlutfall
milli höfðingja, bænda og þræla. Það hlutfall, sem fæst með því að telja saman

14 Barði Guðmundsson (1959) 111. See p. 105.
15 The lack of pagan burials, however, suggests that there might be something dubious about the whole idea of pagan Norsemen dominating most of the
country up to the year 999 when they peacefully decided to become Christian.
But it is not within the scope of the present work to challenge such a well
established consensus.
16 Guðmundur Hannesson (1925).
17 (1946 (1975)) 18. See also Jakob Benediktsson (1968) CXXXII.

29

alla landnemana, sem Landnáma getur um, nær engri átt, og nægir í því
sambandi að minna á, að kynstórir menn eru taldir nær sexfalt fleiri en þrælarn-
ir. En er hægt að hugsa sér nokkurn kynstóran mann, sem ekki hafi átt að
minnsta kosti einn þræl?[18]

Jón Steffensen[19] later worked out a reasonable proportion of
slaves, farmers, wives and settlers. By interpreting all dubious
instances in favour of Gaelic origin (as opposed to Norse as
previous scholars did), he managed, on the basis of *Landnáma*,
to produce results which suggested that as much as 40.7% of the
total population were Gaelic. Of independent settlers and their
free followers he estimated about 13.6% - 25.9% to have
been Gaelic and with 20% of the population being slaves — all
of whom were Gaelic (see p. 30-32) — he ended up with a
reasonable estimation of 30.9% - 40.7% of the first inhabitants in Iceland being Gaelic.[20]

It need not surprise us either that genealogies in the Family
Sagas, many of which are based on *Landnámabók*, are mostly
traced back to chieftains and royal families rather than persons
of "lesser" importance. In societies where people are proud of
their noble ancestry they are very unlikely to record and boast
of for example slaves in their family tree. But though the
sources on the slaves' children are next to non-existing, we have
no real reason to doubt that they were in proportion to the rest
of the population.

It is of interest here to draw attention to a passage in *Þórðar-
bók* (one of the versions of *Landnámabók*), where it says
clearly that Icelanders were accused by foreigners of being

18 "To get sensible results one has to estimate a sound proportion between
chieftains, farmers and slaves. The proportion one derives at by counting all the
settlers mentioned in Landnáma, is absurd, and it is sufficient to point out that
noble men are six times more numerous than the slaves. But is it possible to
think of any noble man who did not at least have one slave?"
19 (1971 (1975)).
20 Ibid, 100.

descendents from slaves and that one reason for writing *Land-náma* is to disprove such accusations:

þat er margra manna mál, at þat sé óskyldr fróðleikr at rita landnám. En vér þykjumsk heldr svara kunna útlendum mǫnnum, þá er þeir bregða oss því, at vér séim komnir af þrælum eða illmennum, ef vér vitum víst várar kynferðir sannar, svá ok þeim mǫnnum, er vita vilja forn frœði eða rekja ættartǫlur, at taka heldr at upphafi til en hǫggvast í mitt mál, enda eru svá allar vitrar þjóðir, at vita vilja upphaf sinna landsbyggða eða hvers<u> hvergi til hefjask eða kynslóðir.[21]

A search for a substantial number of Gaelic people in Iceland must be concentrated on the anonymous masses. It goes without saying that a search of that kind is bound to be extremely speculative but an attempt can be made to find traces of Gaelic presence among the lowest of the low: the slaves.

2.3. Slaves

A considerable number of slaves is believed to have been brought into Iceland from the British Isles, mainly Ireland and Scotland, during the settlement period.[22] It is uncertain how many they were but it has been estimated that the proportion was approximately one slave to every five free men about the

21 336fn. ("People often say that writing about the Settlement is irrelevant learning, but we think we can better meet criticism of foreigners when they accuse us of being descended from slaves or scoundrels, if we know for certain the truth about our ancestry. And for those who want to know ancient lore and how to trace genealogies, it's better to start at the beginning than to come in at the middle. Anyway, all civilized nations want to know about the origins of their own society and the beginnings of their own race." Transl. by Hermann Pálsson and P. Edwards (1972) 6). This passage is believed to be derived from the lost Styrmisbók, dating from the first half of the 13th century. See also Jakob Benediktsson (1968) CIIff.

22 Jón Jóhannesson (1956) 415-16; Björn Þorsteinsson (1966) 127; Jakob Benediktsson (1974) 187-88; Sveinbjörn Rafnsson (1974) 161; Gunnar Karlsson (1975) 25. Peter Foote (1977) 59-60, 72, on the other hand, has argued that slaves were never numerous or important in Iceland.

year 930.[23] Recently, however, it has been suggested that because of great demand for manpower during the settlement period, it is more likely that slaves comprised 30-40% of the population.[24] In the 11th century slavery is considered to have been on the decrease and it is thought to have been totally abrogated in the 12th.[25] It is obvious therefore — whether 20% or 30-40% are accepted as likely figures — that these Irish-Scottish people have made up a larger proportion of the inhabitants than one would have been able to conclude from *Landnámabók* and other written sources.

Irish sources on captives taken by the Vikings may lend support to the idea that many of the slaves in Iceland were of Irish or Scottish extraction. Hermann Pálsson has suggested that Hjǫrleifr's slaves, referred to in *Landnámabók*, may have come from among the "ten hundred" who were carried of or killed in Armagh in 869.[26] Whether this is so or not, it is noteworthy that this is the first record in the Irish annals of a seizure of captives on such a scale.[27] Pictish and Briton slaves are recorded to have been brought to Dublin in great numbers

23 Jón Steffensen (1971 (1975) 100-02. C. Williams (1937) 36, on the other hand, believed that they were by far less numerous and never more than 2000 at any given time.

24 Anna Agnarsdóttir and Ragnar Árnason (1983) 20.

25 Árni Pálsson (1932) 198; Jón Jóhannesson (1956) 419-20; Björn Þorsteinsson (1966) 126-27, 130; Gunnar Karlsson (1975) 26; P. Foote (1977) 69-70. Various views have been put forward to explain why slavery disappeared. See most recently Anna Agnarsdóttir and Ragnar Árnason (1983) and for a summary of previous views, pp.7-15.

26 AU 868 and Hermann Pálsson (1958) 311.

27 A.P. Smyth (1977) 155. Smyth might emphasize the novelty a bit too much. All through the 9th century there are records of captives being taken even though numbers like "ten hundred" are never mentioned (AU 820, "a great number of women"; 830, "great numbers"; 835 "very many captive"; 839, "led away captive bishops and priests and scholars"; 844, "Forannán, abbot of Ard Macha, was taken prisoner by the heathens [...] with his halidoms and following" ("cona muinntir")).

in 871[28] and in "... succeeding years, the mention of great numbers of captives carried off by the Vikings becomes a regular feature of Irish annals."[29] For the rest of the 9th century and during the 10th this newly established custom seems to have flourished and "... was probably much more widespread than even the annals suggest. [...] The absence of any mention of prisoners in the countless notices of the sacking of monasteries and forts does not necessarily mean that no captives were taken."[30] The most successful raid for slaves is recorded in the *Annals of Ulster* under 950:

Gothfrith son of Sitriuc with the foreigners of Áth Cliath plundered Cenannas and Domnach Pátraic and Ard Brecáin and Tuileáin and Cell Scíre and other churches. From Cenannas they were all plundered, and three thousand men or more were taken captive and a great spoil of cattle and horses and gold and silver was taken away.[31]

A.P. Smyth has suggested that the people who were captured in Ireland during this period were far too many for the Icelandic and Scandinavian markets alone.[32] From this it may be concluded that slaves for the Icelandic market were not only easy and cheap to obtain but originated in Ireland.

Since this boom in the slave trade and the colonization of

28 AU 870. Under 865, the AU say that hostages were taken from the "entire Pictish country".

29 A.P. Smyth (1977) 155. See for example entries under the following years where special references are made to captives: AU 870, "a great prey"; 880, "many people"; 894, "seven hundred and ten persons"; 925, "in which many men were killed or captured". AFM 883, "fourteen score persons" — also in *Chronicum Scottorum*, 886; 927 ("undoubtedly with the intention of taking prisoners" — A.P. Smyth (1977) 155).

30 A.P. Smyth (1977) 155.

31 "Gothfrith m. Sitriuc co nGallaibh Atha Cliath do orcain Cenannsa 1 Domnaigh Patraic 1 Aird Breccain 1 Tuileain 1 Cille Scire 1 alailiu cealla olchena. A Cenannus ro orta huile ubi capta sunt tria milia hominum + plus, cum maxima praeda bouum 1 equorum, auri 1 argenti."

32 A.P. Smyth (1977) 159, who also suggests that the surplus was sold "to Islamic societies of the western Mediterranean and the Middle East."

Iceland are contemporaneous, it is tempting to think that there might be a connection between them. It can be suggested that the increased number of slaves available made it easier to break new land in areas like Iceland, thus encouraging colonization of new areas, or: the breaking of new land required more manpower than previously needed, thus encouraging the newly established slave-trade. Either way, it seems quite reasonable to conclude that Icelandic sources are correct in tracing slaves in Iceland to the British Isles, Ireland in particular. It may also be assumed that slavery was the rule rather than the exception (how many the slaves were, remains of course impossible to assess).

If a mass importation of Irish and Scottish slaves to Iceland took place, both the lack of Gaelic names and Gaelic loanwords in Icelandic are explicable. Written evidence suggests that slaves were given Norse names (see. p. 26) and there is no reason to think that their Norwegian or Icelandic masters tolerated the Gaelic language since the slaves were not even allowed to retain their Gaelic names. They would have been obliged to learn Old Norse in order to be able to communicate in that language.

The theory of Irish and Scottish slave immigration may also explain why Gaelic artefacts are not numerous in Iceland, and why domestic animals seem to derive from Scandinavia.[33] All the slaves could bring with them across the sea was themselves. Their work was supervised by Norwegians, and they would have had little opportunity to exert influence on any practical affairs. The only independence they might have been allowed to retain would have related to their attitudes, and perhaps to their methods of entertaining themselves. It is here that literature comes into the picture. As mentioned above, some of the settlers were no doubt familiar with Irish storytelling from their stay in Ireland. They may therefore have developed a taste for such a form of entertainment and encouraged their slaves to tell

33 S. Aðalsteinsson (1981), (1982).

whatever stories they knew, with one possible exception: it is fairly unlikely that a Norwegian would enjoy listening to his slave reciting tales about the heroic deeds of Gaelic heroes — the slave's ancestors. The Norsemen (soon to become Icelanders) must therefore have insisted on tales being told about Scandinavian heroes, rather than Gaelic.

A process along these lines could then provide a channel for Irish storytelling to become a common pastime in Iceland and explain why Gaelic heroes did not find their way into Icelandic literature — a fact which has been used as a major argument against profound Gaelic influence on Icelandic literary tradition.[34]

If a considerable group of Irish or Scottish people came to Iceland, it might be expected that this would have left traces in the physical characteristics of Icelanders. Evidence of this will be discussed in the following chapter.

34 A. Heusler (1913 (1969)) 391, 398-99.

Chapter III

BLOOD GROUPS OF ICELANDERS AND OTHER GENETIC EVIDENCE

A number of traits in which the physique of Icelanders differs from that of the Norwegians have been noted.

Skulls found in Iceland from before the year 1000 differ considerably from those found in Norway but show certain similarities to skulls found in the British Isles. Due to scarcity of evidence however, it is difficult to conclude whether the skulls in question can be looked upon as representative for the general mass of people. It has nevertheless been suggested from skull measurements that Icelanders might be the result of a mixture between Norwegian and Gaelic people.[1]

The distribution of ABO, MN and Rhesus blood groups in Iceland was investigated in the early fifties. It was shown that O group is most common in Iceland, Scotland and Ireland but A is the least frequent, whereas the reverse is true in Norway. The distribution of MN and Rhesus groups, however, did not appear to be distinctive from the rest of Western Europe.[2] From this evidence, Donegani et al.[3] concluded that people from Scotland and Ireland were probably more numerous among the first settlers in Iceland than generally believed. As a further support

1 Jón Steffensen (1946 (1975)) 25, (1951 (1975)) 37-42. Also A.C. Berry (1974) who, on the basis of skull measurements, found that the Icelanders were closer to the people of the Orkneys and Shetland than to Norwegians. This gets further support from a recent study of certain HLA genetic markers which strongly suggests a close connection between Iceland and the Hebrides (Alfreð Árnason PhD, The Blood Bank of Iceland — personal communication).

2 J.A. Donegani et al. (1950); Ásmundur Brekkan (1954).

3 (1950) 150-51.

they also pointed out that "the Icelanders are darker [than Scandinavians] and can by no means be described as a fair-haired people. The percentage of redhaired people is definitely higher than among the Scandinavians."[4]

Recently, however, much more detailed genetic analyses have been undertaken in order to investigate the proportions of Norwegian and Gaelic people in the making of the Icelandic nation. The distribution of the ABO blood groups has been confirmed. On that evidence alone, "the calculated proportion of Norwegian genes is still below 25%."[5] Another study, based on "five serological loci"[6] and taking "a stochastic element (random genetic drift) into the determination of the true population gene frequencies"[7] suggests an almost wholly Gaelic origin for the Icelandic nation.[8] Further, it has been noted that the frequency of Phenylketonuria (Following's disease) in Iceland as well as "gene frequencies in several genetic marker systems including the rhesus, Kell and PGM1 systems"[9] resembles that of Ireland and differs considerably from that of Norway, thus demonstrating that fewer than 25% of the first inhabitants of Iceland were of Norwegian descent.[10]

Apparently, these conclusions are not as straightforward as they seem.

First, the argument presupposes that the present inhabitants of the countries in question are direct descendants of the inhabitants a thousand years ago, and secondly that the gene frequency has not changed very much, either through natural

4 Ibid, 150.
5 O. Bjarnason et al. (1973) 448.
6 E.A. Thompson (1973) 77.
7 Ibid, 80.
8 Ibid, 77-79.
9 L.F. Saugstad (1977) 60.
10 Ibid, 60. See also "Comments" by various authors, on Saugstad's article, both in the same volume, pp. 66-83 and in vol. 11, pp. 57-60. These comments are supplemented by a useful bibliography on genetic studies.

selection or through genetic drift, from the time of settlement in Iceland.

Since no mass migrations are known to have taken place, the first assumption must be regarded as reasonable. The second one has received more attention and requires further discussion.

It is possible that plagues and various diseases in Iceland have affected the gene frequencies and thus caused major changes through natural selection during a period of 1000 years. Stefán Aðalsteinsson has argued in favour of this by suggesting that "the low frequency of A and high frequency of O blood group genes in the Icelandic human population is the result of a selective disadvantage of A during severe smallpox epidemics." [11]

Previous authors however, had argued that Iceland was not different from its neighbouring countries in terms of epidemics, diseases, and other external factors. [12] The only obvious difference would lie in the volcanic activity in Iceland but it is not clear how that should affect the genes. [13] Another peculiarity in Iceland could be the high frequency of "carcinoma of the stomach and hydatid disease. [But it] is unlikely that gastric

11 (1985) 275. Stefán Aðalsteinsson is somewhat misleading in his article when he says that the evidence of ABO blood gene frequencies stands alone against the evidence of "written sources, language, culture and farm animals" (276) which is all said to point to a Scandinavian origin of the Icelanders. As is pointed out below this is not entirely true since the ABO evidence adds to the likelihood of what is suspected from the historical evidence. In addition to that, Icelandic culture is radically different from the Norwegian one in aspects where it shows close affinities with the Irish and Scottish. Furthermore it seems irrelevant to mention the origin of farm animals in this context (see also p. 33). The calculations which serve to show how the present-day West Norwegian ABO blood gene frequencies could be changed into the present-day Icelandic ones seem to be based on several assumptions about the effects of small-pox in Norway and Iceland respectively. A more detailed research would therefore be needed before the available evidence can be used.

12 E.A. Thompson (1973) 69; O. Bjarnason et al. (1973) 429-31.

13 O. Bjarnason et al. (1973) 431.

carcinoma could have had a very marked influence on the genetic structure in the time available as most of those afflicted would have completed their families."[14]

Possible natural change or drift through a long period of time is of course difficult to assess. It has been argued, however, that if any considerable drift or change took place, it is very unlikely that all the factors involved would have developed in the same direction, so as to give such — apparently — unanimous results.[15]

In a recent article E.M. Wijsman[16] has introduced a new method to use the available statistics on gene frequencies. From her calculations it seems that the standard deviations are such that no definite conclusions can be drawn. By making sveral assumptions however, about drift and sampling error she estimates that 86% were of Norwegian origin and 14% of Irish. Her results also indicate that the ABO frequencies "give abnormal estimates of admixture compared to other loci."[17]

Even if some of these methods are accepted as reliable, the results can be interpreted in different ways. It has for example been suggested that there was a distinctive tribe in Norway which was especially active in Viking raids in the West and later in the settlement of Iceland.[18] This tribe is then seen as of an older breed in Europe which now only survives on the outskirts of the continent and in other isolated places (e.g. Basques, Corsicans, Sardinians, Walsers of the high Alps etc.). People in these areas all show high frequencies of O blood group but since they differ considerably in Rh and MN blood groups — which appear to be even more stable than ABO groups — there is "no question of close relationship between the various populations."[19]

14 Ibid.
15 E.A. Thompson (1973) 69.
16 (1984).
17 Ibid, 441.
18 Jón Steffensen (1951* (1975)), (1969 (1975)).
19 O. Bjarnason et al. (1973) 452.

Another, highly speculative, explanation is that the genetical composition of migratory groups is different from those who choose to stay at home. Emigrants could be "genetically restless", thus explaining the difference between Iceland and Norway.[20] All these qualifications must be born in mind when interpreting the biological evidence. Unfortunately, I am in no position to take any stand in a learned discussion on human genetics. But, to a layman, it seems, from the resemblances mentioned above, that the obvious and most simple way to interpret the biological evidence is to say that it adds to the likelihood of what was already strongly suspected from the historical evidence, i.e. that a substantial number of Gaelic people were among the first inhabitants of Iceland.[21]

It need not, however, be necessary to accept the conclusions which suggest a totally Gaelic origin, bearing in mind that there are factors which show a close relationship with Norway and have not been accounted for.[22] But since most of the evidence points in the same direction, it should be relatively safe to argue that at least 14%, but more likely even more, were of Gaelic origin and thus by far exceeding the results we are likely to get from counting Gaelic names in written sources, such as *Landnámabók*. The question now is not about the very small percentage which Craigie and Finnur Jónsson (see p. 23 and 27) were prepared to admit when they argued against any substantial Gaelic influence in Iceland. Our present knowledge has

20 R.J. Berry (1977) 67.
21 See e.g. E.A. Thompson (1978) 57-58: "From a statistician's viewpoint the simplest hypothesis is the best. Unless selection is found, there is no need to invoke it to explain what can be more simply explained by a largely Celtic origin for the Icelanders."
22 R.J. Berry (1977) 67, who says, referring to O. Bjarnason et al. (1973): "... there are a number of genetical systems where the "Norwegian frequency" [...] is closer to the Icelandic one than is the Irish one. This applies to the rhesus and acid phophatase loci in particular. [...] It is unfortunate that we know so little about the factors influencing gene frequencies in man."

given the discussion a totally different complexion: it is now not so much a question of how large a part we can assign to the Gaelic element, but rather where on the scale fram 2% upwards the Norwegian contribution can be placed. But for the purpose of allowing for substantial Gaelic influence on Icelandic culture, the moderate suggestion of 14-40% seems more than adequate.

Chapter IV

LATER CONTACTS BETWEEN ICELAND AND THE GAELIC WORLD ON THE ORKNEYS

4.1. The Nature of the Contacts

A possible route for Gaelic motifs and stories to reach Iceland, was via the Orkneys. In recent years both M. Chesnutt[1] and Bo Almqvist[2] have emphasised the importance of the Orkneys as an intermediary between the Gaelic and Icelandic cultures:

> It [i.e. the Orkneys] stood on the fringes of the Gaelic-speaking area, but was constantly in touch with Iceland. Icelandic authors had no other means of access to *bilingual* literary tradition.[3]

This is of course true as far it goes. The Orkneys were probably a channel through which motifs could travel in both directions. But contacts of this kind would hardly have been sufficient to cause or encourage a radical change in Icelandic culture. If any major influence is postulated with the Orkneys as a point of contact we are again faced with the same problem as A. Heusler (see p. 50) drew attention to, arguing against the Viking-saga hypothesis: Why did this influence not have similar effects in Norway or the Scandinavian colonies in the west? The

1 (1968).
2 (1981)
3 M. Chesnutt (1968) 129.

42

Orkneys were closely linked with Norway as well as with Iceland.

It is therefore more likely that cultural contacts and exchanges which took place on the Orkneys between Icelandic and Gaelic-speaking people were limited to single motifs, tales or poems. This does not mean that these single features are limited in number, only that they are found as single items in a tradition which had to be built up within Iceland from the cultural elements available in the country itself.

As examples for motifs of this kind attention may be drawn to some of these mentioned in the above-mentioned articles.[4] The discussion will, however, be limited to motifs which travelled to Iceland. Scandinavian impact on Gaelic folklore is not within the scope of the present work.

4.2. The "Everlasting Fight" — Hjaðningavíg

The "Everlasting Fight" motif is common in Irish tradition. Sometimes the otherworld chiefs fight continuously until a human being intervenes and concludes the battle; other accounts tell of the slain rising from death every morning etc. The motif was probably known "in Scandinavia before the Viking Age in the Hild-legend, but there are so many and varied versions of this motif in Iceland that they could not all be attributed to that legend."[5]

4 Bo Almqvist (1981) makes it clear that: "We should not, of course, imagine that the Orkney Earldom was always an intermediary in the exchange of such tales. There was also a direct Gaelic influence on West Scandinavian, especially Icelandic and Faroese, folk tradition, since some of the Scandinavian settlers on these islands came via Ireland and Scotland and had sometimes lived there and absorbed Gaelic culture." 89.

5 Einar Ólafur Sveinsson (1959) 17. See pp. 17-18 for references in Irish and Icelandic traditions. Also F. Panzer (1901) 154-82. Einar Ólafur Sveinsson thinks that 'Celtic' tales must have played an important part in forming Icelandic ideas about the everlasting fight — a motif which becomes extremely common in Iceland, right down to the 19th century, but is rare in Scandinavian tradition.

Háttalykill, a *clavis metrica* composed in the Orkneys in the 1140s by an Icelander and the Orkney Earl Rǫgnvaldr kali, contains what is believed to be the earliest reference to the "Everlasting Fight" motif[6] in Old Norse/Icelandic literature.[7] This motif later became more common in Iceland and there seems to be little doubt that it reached the North from the Gaelic world.[8] Chesnutt[9] has drawn attention to an Irish text, possibly from the eleventh century in its present form, *Cath Maige Turedh,* which tells of a continuous fight and shows, if nothing else, that the motif is old enough to have influenced the *Háttalykill.*

Three of the motifs as they appear in Snorri's version show considerable similarities to the Irish story, namely "the magic sword, the resuscitation of men, and the repair of weapons during the night. A less obvious point of comparison, but one which should surely be registered, is the participation of a woman in the magic rites. The wizard's daughter in Irish answers to the princess Hild in Norse."[10] And later he says:

According to *Cath Maige Turedh,* the Tuatha Dé Danann enjoy three magic advantages. Their wizard can revive the dying; their weapons are "reborn overnight"; and their druidesses can create an army out of *stones* or other raw material. In *Skáldskaparmál,* we are first told that the princess raised the fallen. Later it is added that the men and weapons on the battlefield were turned to stone, only to regain their former shape next day. Snorri separates these

---

6 Or the "Resuscitating Hag" motif as Bo Almqvist (1981) 93, suggests it should be called since one of the characteristics of these stories is that a hag revives the fallen.

7 M. Chesnutt (1968) 130-131, also discusses a reference in *Ragnarsdrápa* by Bragi Boddason inn gamli ("the Old" - see pp. 103-04) used by Snorri Sturluson in his *Skáldskaparmál* (ch.62) as an authority on Hjaðningar. But *Ragnarsdrápa* does not link the Hjaðningar with the Everlasting fight. This is first done in the *Háttalykill.* Chesnutt suggests that Snorri had little but these poetic sources for his treatment of the motif.

8 See Bo Almqvist (1981) 92-3 M. Chestnutt (1968) 131, and references in these works.

9 (1968) 131 ff.

10 M. Chesnutt (1968) 132.

statements, as though uncertain of their joint meaning. If the distinct elements found in the Irish version were allusively handled (or already confused) in his poetic sources, we can understand his bewilderment.[11]

In connection with this idea it may be mentioned that in both traditions we come across stories about monster cats and cats which put their paws into the mouths of slain warriors in order to revive them. "This motif is also of Celtic origin."[12]

But the "Everlasting Fight" or the "Resuscitating Hag" motif must have travelled to the North by more routes than this Orkney poem alone. Otherwise an addition to the motif which can only be found in Iceland and the Gaelic area but not in Scandinavia could hardly be explained.

In some Irish oral tales (and perhaps in Scottish Gaelic ones too, but this I have not investigated) one also finds the notion that only a mortal man can put an end to an "everlasting" fight in the fairy world. This motif, which is found in *Högna þáttr* (and elsewhere in Old Icelandic literature) is also likely to have been borrowed by the Norsemen from the Gaels. Within Scandinavia it does not seem to have spread outside Iceland.[13]

This is not to say, however that the Orkneys did not play an important role in the transmission of this motif. The very fact that the Hjaðningavíg are located on the islands shows that the story was probably associated with them in some way.

One other example from Bo Almqvist's article[14] will suffice to show that even though the Orkneys were an ideal meeting place where the two cultures could exchange traditions, the Gaelic customs in question did often exist in Iceland as well, originating there from Gaels among the settlers. It is another matter that these traditions could be reinforced because of contacts in the Orkneys.

11 Ibid, 132.
12 Einar Ólafur Sveinsson (1959) 18. See there for further references.
13 Bo Almqvist (1981) 93-4.
14 Ibid, 97ff.

4.3. *Orkneyinga saga* — *Severed Heads*

In *Orkneyinga saga* (ch.5), Sigurðr, the first Earl of Orkney, defeats a Scottish Earl, Melbrikta (nicknamed "tönn" — tooth), in battle, cuts his and his followers' heads off, attaches them to his saddle and gallops triumphantly away. Unfortunately for Sigurðr, Melbrikta's tooth, sticking out of the severed head's mouth, wounds Sigurðr's calf, causing a deadly infection. The very custom of using heads as a token of triumph and even hanging them on horses was common enough among the Celts, examples of which can be found in numerous sources.[15] This also recalls numerous references in Icelandic sources about a head-cult of some sort and related folkbeliefs. Many of these are believed to be due to Gaelic influence and some are so well established that they are most likely to have developed within Iceland (see also pp. 81-2).

The distinctive element in *Orkneyinga saga*, however, is that the head-episode is connected with revenge. An Old Irish parallel to this combination of motifs can be found in *Aided Chonchobuir*. In this story a ball made out of the brain of a Leinster king, Mesgegra, and used by the Ulstermen to boast about their victory, is stolen by a Connachtman and eventually thrown at the Ulster king, Conchobhar MacNessa. The ball enters his head but does not cause his death until several years later, when Conchobhar receives the news of Christ's crucifixion. Then the ball falls out of his head, leaving a hole for the blood to gush forth, whereupon Conchobhar dies, is baptized in his own blood and becomes the first Irishman to go straight to Heaven.

The pattern of revenge is rather complicated in the Irish story and not as straightforward as in *Orkneyinga saga* where the

15 See H.M. & N.K. Chadwick (1932) 92-4; N.K. Chadwick (1970) 49-50; K.H. Jackson (1964) 19-20.

full-sized head kills the actual killer, soon after being separated from the body. The similarities nevertheless lead Bo Almqvist to conclude:

One need not assume that the tale about Mesgegra's brain is the direct source of the Melbrikta episode in *Orkneyinga saga,* but some such Gaelic story, perhaps in a more primitive form and without the hagiographic ingredients, seems likely to lie behind it.[16]

4.4. Miscellaneous

4.4.1. Darraðarljóð and Krákumál

More typical, however, of the literary products which are likely to have emerged from the cultural mixture on the Orkneys and the Scottish Isles are poems such as *Darraðarljóð* and *Krákumál.* These have been shown, beyond doubt it may be said, in various works[17] to have been composed on these islands.

Evidence of contacts between the Gaelic and Scandinavian worlds in the 12th and 13th centuries can also be drawn from *Konungs-Skuggsjá* which was written in Norway.

4.4.2. Konungs Skuggsjá

Konungs Skuggsjá contains a passage on Ireland which shows similarities to *Topographia Hibernica* of Giraldus Cambrensis. It has been claimed that these similarities should be explained by a written source[18] even though some scholars maintain that name forms in *Konungs Skuggsjá* reflect Irish pronunciation of

16 (1981) 99.
17 Mainly by A. Holtsmark (1939) and references there (also same author (1957)); and Magnus Olsen (1935) and references there.
18 A. Holtsmark (1964).

the 13th century, thus pointing to oral transmission of the stories.[19]

M. Chesnutt[20] has argued that the passage (whether its source was written or oral) testifies to relations between Ireland and Norway in the 13th century and he suggests that these were through ecclesiastical contacts, mainly on the evidence of a cult connected with St. Olaf in Ireland and Irish stories being attached to him in Norway (see on the Masterbuilder, pp.65-6). Elaborating on this possibility, Chesnutt says that Latin would "have been the medium of communication"[21] thus allowing for Irish elements to reach Iceland, not only orally during the settlement period, but also at a later stage when some of them "may have been taken over from the literature of the church."[22]

4.4.3. Battle of Clontarf

Njáls saga and Þorsteins saga Síðu-Hallssonar contain accounts of Brjánsbardagi (Battle of Clontarf). S. Bugge[23] thought that these were based on a saga, written in Ireland in the early 11th century. The evidence for this, however, is very slim and later scholars have been more inclined to postulate a saga, written in Iceland about the year 1200 and based on oral stories from the West, and later incorporated into Njáls saga and Þorsteins saga Síðu-Hallssonar.[24]

These examples indicate that what was passed on to Iceland via the Orkneys can not be regarded as having a great impact on the literary culture there. Konungs Skuggsjá also shows that Norway was equally open to this influence, which, however, did not have any significant consequences for literary development in medieval Norway.

19. K. Meyer (1984); J. Young (1938). See for the most recent discussion on the Irish marvels in Konungs Skuggsjá, W. Sayers (1985).
20 (1968) 125-6.
21 Ibid, 126.
22 Ibid.
23 (1908) 65.
24 Einar Ólafur Sveinsson (1954) xlv-xlix; A.J. Goedheer (1938).

Chapter V

FORNALDARSÖGUR NORÐURLANDA

5.1. *Late Writing of Older Oral Stories*

The writing of *Fornaldarsögur* (FAS) is generally believed to have started at the end of the Literary Golden Age in Iceland in the late 13th century and become increasingly popular in the 14th century when most of them are thought to have been written down.[1]

The appearance of the genre is connected with the arrival in Iceland of translations of French romances which caused a change in literary taste and made stories of the FAS-type acceptable as written literature in a *milieu* where the realistic approach of the Family and Kings' Sagas had been dominant hitherto.[2]

The FAS are prose narratives containing occasional poems. Some are retellings of old Germanic legends, others are concerned with the Vikings, and a third category contains more general folktale motifs.[3]

They are set in Scandinavia and more distant countries, in a period before the settlement of Iceland and some of them have an amount of basis in reality in so far as they refer to historical characters or events which are known to have taken place,

---

1 Guðni Jónsson (1959) XII; Einar Ólafur Sveinsson (1959*); (1965) 161-63; Finnur Jónsson (1923) gives more credit to the second half of the 13th century whereas "enkelte er vistnok først skrevne i det 14. árh." (787) ("some are probably first written in the 14th century.").

2 Sigurður Nordal (1953 (1968)) 100-02.

3 Einar Ólafur Sveinsson (1959) 15.

though FAS can by no means be labelled as a historical genre.[4] What is most characteristic of the genre, however, is how the stories:

... display a great love of the supernatural, magic, spells, trolls and dwarfs. There the supernatural has lost the resemblance of folk-belief, as fantastic elements now prevail.[5]

The change in literary taste brought about by the French romances has been seen as opening up a channel for Gaelic motifs into Icelandic literature, the FAS in particular. These motifs are supposed to have survived orally in Iceland for centuries until they became acceptable to the literary elite, from the 13th century onwards. Finally, in this late genre, "Celtic motifs emerge in great numbers."[6]

It is rather difficult to accept that single Gaelic motifs are supposed to have survived for centuries before surfacing in literature. Motifs usually form a part of a story and since the motifs in question are most common in the FAS, it seems plausible to suggest that the FAS represent the type of stories which Gaelic people told during the Age of Settlement when they adapted their stories and narrative technique to a Scandinavian setting and Scandinavian characters.[7]

It seems an unnecessary complication to explain the change in literary taste as a result of French influence (unless all that is

4 Guðni Jónsson (1959) XIIIff.

5 Einar Ólafur Sveinsson (1959) 15-16.

6 Einar Ólafur Sveinsson (1959) 16. See also same author (1932).

7 Einar Ólafur Sveinsson (1959) 16, seems to think along the same lines when he says: "We see now that Celtic stories must have been handed down orally, especially among the lower classes of the community. Now a literary taste, which causes them to be brought to the surface and reduced to writing has gained the upper hand." Einar Ólafur Sveinsson does not, however, see this as having been of any major significance for literary development in the country. It is also hard to see where the "lower classes" come into the picture unless we regard the guests at the Reykjahólar-wedding and King Sverrir (see p. 51-2) as members of the lower classes!

meant by French influence is that it provided the stimulus for people to write down stories which already existed orally). The literary taste was already there and it is more likely that stories of this kind were receptive to motifs from French romances than vice versa.

It has of course often been suggested that the FAS represent what is called "Viking-Sagas", a saga genre believed to have arisen under Gaelic influence among Vikings in the west and spread to Scandinavia and Iceland in the 11th century. In Iceland these "Viking-Sagas" are then seen as playing an important role in the literary development.[8] In view of what was said earlier, however, it is unlikely that the Vikings in the west could have been influenced to such an extent at this early date.

A.Heusler[9] discussed the Viking-Saga hypothesis at some length and brought forward three major arguments against it. First that Sagas were written only in Iceland and not in Scandinavia or in the colonies in the west. Secondly that no Irish Saga has been preserved in Iceland and thirdly that in the development of Saga-literature in Iceland the Family and Kings' Sagas are generally seen as coming first.

Heusler's first objection can be overcome if the Gaelic influence giving rise to the FAS is seen as taking place in Iceland during the Age of Settlement (see p. 33). The second one has already been dealt with (see p. 34) but the third point requires more discussion.

The evidence for a late date for the writing of the FAS is rather slight and mainly based on the assumption that they were written under influence from French romances which reached Iceland at a late stage. If, however, the FAS are seen as representing the oldest Saga-form in Iceland — on the grounds that they contain the oldest material, both Scandinavian and Gaelic, which must have reached Iceland in the Age of Settlement, and

8 A. Olrik (1907 (1925)) 124-42; A. Bugge (1908); (1916).

9 (1913 (1969)) 391ff. For a most convenient summary of this argument, see T.M. Andersson (1964) 56-61.

that the earliest references to storytelling in Iceland are to tales of the FAS-type (see below) — they need no longer be seen as a late offshoot, and this implies that the traditional view · about the writing of the FAS must be reconsidered. The Viking-Saga hypothesis was totally rejected by Finnur Jónsson[10] and has not been much discussed since. The present argument, however, owes something to these earlier theories but the basic difference is that here the development is seen as taking place within Iceland.

It may of course be argued that the FAS are purely literary products and the Gaelic motifs reached Iceland via the French romances. But it will be shown below that many of the Gaelic motifs in question are most likely to be derived directly from Gaelic tradition and there is overwhelming evidence to suggest that the FAS flourished at an early stage, most likely in an oral form.

5.1.1. Evidence of Oral Fornaldarsögur

The earliest reference we have to story-telling in Iceland is in an often quoted passage in *Þorgils saga ok Hafliða*.[11] Here we hear of a wedding held at Reykjahólar in 1119 where a saga

frá Hröngviði víkingi ok frá Óláfi Liðsmannakonungi ok haugbroti Þráins berserks ok Hrómundi Gripssyni — ok margar vísur með[12]

was told. And

Ingimundur prestr sagði sögu Orms Barreyiarskálds ok vísur margar ok flokk góðan við enda sögunnar, er Ingimundur hafði ortan.[13]

10 e.g. (1923) 785.

11 In *Sturlunga saga* I, 12-50, see esp. 23ff.

12 Ibid, 27 ("about Hröngvið the viking and about Óláf, the Liðsmen's King, about the barrow-robber, Þráin the berserk, and about Hrómund Gripsson - with many strophes too" — transl. by J.H. McGrew (1974) 44).

13 Ibid, 27("Ingimund the priest told the Saga of Orm the Skáld of Barra, with many verses and, towards the end of the saga, many good *flokkrs* which Ingimund himself had composed." Transl. by J.H. McGrew (1974) 44).

52

About the first saga we are told:

þessari sögu var skemmt Sverri konungi, ok kallaði hann slíkar lygisögur skemmtiligstar.[14]

Orms saga Barreyjarskálds is now lost and so is the original *Hrómundar saga Gripssonar.* The contents of the latter work, however, is preserved in the form of a metrical romance or *rímur*, entitled *Griplur*, believed to follow the lost saga fairly closely.[15]

One version of *Landnáma*[16] refers to a saga about King Vatnarr being told (possibly before 1100[17]) and two of his sons, Sniallr and Hialldr, are mentioned. These characters appear in one FAS, *Hálfs saga ok Hálfsrekka*, but a separate saga of King Vatnarr has not survived.

The earliest reference which is generally accepted to be to a written FAS is from 1263 when Sturla Þórðarson visited the Norwegian king, Magnús lagabætir.[18] Sturla first entertains the ship's crew with *Huldar saga*, which is now lost but appears to have contained FAS material. He is later invited by the queen to come to her residence "ok hafa með sér tröllkonusöguna."[19]

14 Ibid, 27 ("These sagas delighted King Sverri who said such lying stories were very enjoyable," Transl. by J.H. McGrew (1974) 44). Hermann Pálsson (1962) 49ff, has argued, contrary to most scholars, that the sagas used for entertainment at the wedding were already written down. He bases his argument on a reference in Snorri's *Ólafs saga helga* (Prologus), saying that the writing of sagas in Iceland started about 240 years after the beginning of settlement in Iceland, i.e. about 1110, and a reference in *Þorgils saga ok Hafliða* about *Hrómundar saga Gripssonar*: "Þessa sögu hafði Hrólfr sjálfr saman setta." ("Hrólf himself had put this saga together." Transl. by J.H. McGrew (1974) 44). "Setja saman sögu", according to Hermann Pálsson, always refers to writing and is a translation or the equivalent of the Latin *componere*.

15 See Einar Ólafur Sveinson (1959*).

16 *Skarðsárbók* (Viðauki) 191-92.

17 Finnur Jónsson (1923) 785.

18 "Sturlu þáttr" in *Sturlunga saga* II, 227-36, esp. 232-33.

19 Ibid, 233.

The reference to bringing "the troll-woman saga with him" clearly indicates that it was written down at the time.[20] Further support for the existence of the FAS in oral tradition at an early date may be found in Saxo Grammaticus (about 1200). Saxo refers to Icelanders as his main informants (see p. iv) and uses many FAS, characters from which appear in Icelandic FAS later on, even though their separate sagas have not survived in all instances.[21] Existing manuscripts of the FAS date mostly from about 1400 onwards but a few can be dated earlier. One page not younger than 1300 has survived with an episode from *Hrólfs saga Gautrekssonar* (AM 567 4to, XIV), and *Örvar-Odds saga* is contained in a manuscript from 1325-50 (Sth. 7, 4to). Neither of these manuscripts is believed to be an original.[22]

The dates of manuscripts, however, tells but little of the age of the original written saga. The Family and Kings' Sagas are mostly preserved in manuscripts later than 1300 even though they were most likely written down during the 13th century. But the actual writing down of the FAS is not of major importance if they are regarded as being based on oral prose narratives, close to the earliest prose narratives ever told in Iceland. As such, they must have played a significant role in the forming of an oral prose narrative tradition in the country, regardless of the time at which they were written. The hypothesis that Gaelic influence is very strong in the FAS depends on such an assumption about the origins of the genre.

5.2. Gaelic Influence in the Fornaldarsögur

Instances of Gaelic influence which have been pointed out in the FAS and related works, can be grouped in two main

20 Ibid, 310, note II. 5 where it is also suggested that this may have been a misunderstanding by the queen. See also Hermann Pálsson (1962) 168-69.
21 See A. Olrik (1894) and Guðni Jónsson (1959) X-XII.
22 See Finnur Jónsson (1923) 786-87.

54

categories. First there is general influence of ideas and beliefs where single motifs have not been borrowed but the similarities:

[...] appear rather to be common themes, developing independently in the two countries, Ireland and Scandinavia or Iceland, but sufficiently close to suggest a close relationship in origin. The same supernatural themes are current, and the same spiritual forces are emphasised in both the early Celtic and the early Northern world.[23]

Secondly, single motifs can be looked for and traced to Irish, Scottish or Welsh stories.

5.2.1. General resemblances

5.2.1.1. Rebirth

Ideas on rebirth in Irish and Icelandic traditions show certain similarities. An example of the Irish can be found in a story called *Tochmarc Étaíne*. [24] In Icelandic the most complete story about rebirth concerns Helgi and Sigrún in the Helgi poems in the *Poetic Edda*. Belief in rebirth also seems to appear in the FAS, if we accept N.K. Chadwick's plausible view[25] that Helgi and his mistress Lára in *Hrómundar saga Gripssonar* are to be identified with Helgi Haddingjaskati and Kára who are said to

23 N.K. Chadwick (1957) 177-78. She claims that the general nature of the FAS is very similar to the earliest Irish tales from the *Cín Dromma Snechta* (a now lost manuscript, probably written sometime in the 8th to 10th centuries. (See R. Thurneysen (1921) 16 and (1936) 218; G. Murphy (1952) 144ff.) Its contents may be deduced by references to it in other manuscripts, esp. *Lebor na hUidre* and *The Book of Leinster*).

24 See further in *De Chophur in da Muccida*. Examples of rebirth in Irish are extremely common. See A. Nutt (1895-1897) who also points out Scandinavian parallels.

25 (1957) 180-81.

55

have been Helgi and Sigrún reborn and told of in the now lost
Káruljóð [26]
At first sight, the dissimilarities between these stories are the
most obvious. In the Irish, the woman, Étaín, keeps her name
for three generations and marries different men whereas in the
Icelandic, identical pairs re-marry even though it is only the
male, Helgi, who retains his name. In spite of this radical
difference, attention has been drawn to some peculiar
similarities:

It is remarkable that in both the Irish and the Norse stories the brother of the
hero has love relations with the hero's wife, and that the hero, so far from
resenting such a union, gives it his blessing. In both stories the heroine is seen in
the air in the form of a swan before her final disappearance. [27]

Eochaid, Étaín's husband, leaves Étaín and Ailill, his
brother, at home. Ailill is madly in love with Étaín but is
"cured" of his desire. Eochaid has no objections. This is re-
miniscent of how Héðinn, brother of Helgi, falls in love with
Helgi's wife, Svava, regrets this immediately but is forgiven by
Helgi who on his deathbed asks Héðinn to marry Svava
(*Helgakviða Hjörvarðssonar*). Helgi and Svava are later reborn
as are Eochaid and Étaín. Lára's (Sigrún's/Svava's) final appearance was mentioned above. Étaín, however, is transformed

26 See *Helgakviða Hundingsbana II*. The passage in *Hrómundar saga*,
containing the final reference to them reads: "Helgi frækni hafði jafnan sigr
haft ok vann með fjölkynngi. Frilla hans hét Lára, sú sem þar var í álftarlíki.
Helgi reiddi svá hátt sverð sitt upp yfir sik, at þat tók sundr fótlegg álftarinnar,
ok renndi sverðit ofan í völlinn upp at hjöltum, ok mælti: "Nú er mín heill farin,
ok illa tókst til, er ek missta þín." "(ch. 7) ("Helgi the brave had always been
victorious by means of magic. His mistress who was there in the shape of a swan
was called Lára. Helgi lifted his sword so high up over his head that it severed
the leg of the swan, and he plunged the sword down into the ground right up to
the cross-pieces and said: "Now my fortune is at an end and it went ill when I
lost you."") For a further discussion on Icelandic beliefs in rebirth, see N.K.
Chadwick (1957) 179ff. And S. Bugge (1896) 305 ff.
27 N.K. Chadwick (1957) 182.

into a swan to be able to elope from Eochaid with her former
husband, Midir.

5.2.1.2. Rebirth and Barrows

Barrows play an important role in connection with rebirth
and life after death. In *Flateyjarbók,* the early half-legendary
Norwegian king, Ólafr Geirstaða-Álfr, is said to have been
reborn as St. Ólafr, king of Norway in the 11th century. The
rebirth is made possible by a visit to Ólafr Geirstaða-Álfr's
gravemound where his head is cut off the corpse.[28] St. Ólafr
himself is reported to have experienced a feeling of *déjà vu*
when paying a visit to the mound but is much embarrassed when
he denies ever having said anything to that effect.[29]

A parallel may be found in an Irish story from the *Cín
Dromma Snechta* where King Mongan of Antrim is accused by
a warrior of the Fenians who appears from the dead, of being
Finn macCumaill reborn. Mongan tries to ignore the accusa-
tion but the saga-writer makes clear that this was in fact the
case.[30]

These similarities must be looked at in connection with related beliefs about mounds and otherworld adventures.

5.2.1.3. Barrows and Journeys to the Otherworld

N.K. Chadwick[31] has looked at and compared the function of
the *síd* and *haugr* in Irish, Welsh and Icelandic traditions. She
points out that sitting on a barrow is "the recognized way to

28 See *Flateyjarbók II* (þáttr Ólafs Geirstaða-Álfs in *Ólafs saga hins helga*)
7-9.

29 Ibid, 135.

30 Ed. in *Lebor na hUidre,* 334-35. For a translation, see T.P. Cross and
C.H. Slover (1969) 548-50.

31 (1957).

experience a marvel in both Norse and Welsh literature."[32] As examples of this she refers to the Welsh Pwyll who is seated on the mound of Arberth[33] and told that he "can not leave it without first receiving wounds or blows, or else seeing a marvel."[34]

Similar ideas seem to be behind the story of Helgi (in *Helgakviða Hjörvarðssonar*) in which he sits on a mound and sees valkyries, one of whom is later to become his wife.[35]

The mounds, especially the Irish *síd* are also connected with "The Land of the Living"[36] which brings us to a series of similar ideas in the two traditions in connection with visits to the otherworld and supernatural fosterages.

Irish tradition is rich in stories about people going to the "Land of the Living" or the otherworld.[37]

Connla the Fair is called upon by a lady who gives him an apple to eat and appears later to bring him away across the sea.[38]

The Voyage of Bran son of Febal is an example of this as well. There a woman calls on Bran and his followers who set out for the promised land. When they return after what they think is only three years, ages have passed, and one crew-member who sets his foot on Irish soil, immediately turns into dust.

32 Ibid, 180.
33 *Pwyll Prince of Dyfed* in *The Mabinogion*, 3-24.
34 N.K. Chadwick (1957) 180fn.
35 For Icelandic examples of sitting on a mound, see A. Olrik (1909).
36 "This is the *óðáinsakr*, the *Jörð Lifandi Manna* of Norse, the *undensakre* of Saxo, *Tír Tairngeri*, *Tír Béo* of Irish." (N.K. Chadwick (1957) 198).
37 These are called *echtrae* and *immrama* (adventures and voyages). See M. Dillon (1969) 101-31.
38 *Echtra Connla macCuinn*. This story is believed to have been in *Cín Dromma Snechta*. For this and the following, see N.K. Chadwick (1957) 192ff. A peculiar echo of the apple-motif appears in the Icelandic *Völsunga saga* ch. 2. There the childless king Rerir is meditating on a mound when a maiden appears to him. She gives him an apple which he later eats with his wife. Soon afterwards, they have a son - an ancestor of Sigurd the Dragon-slayer. They themselves die immediately.

58

Echtra Nerai tells of a man who visits a *síd* and falls in love there. After a short come-back to the "normal" world, he goes to the *síd*, never to be seen again.

In Icelandic, *Eiríks saga víðförla* tells of Eiríkr's journey to the Ódáinsakr, his return to his own people and ten years later his final and sudden disappearance.[39] Helgi Þórisson has a similar fate. He falls in love with an otherworld woman at the court of Goðmundr á Glæsivöllum and is only granted a short visit back (see *Helga þáttr Þórissonar*). Einar Ólafur Sveinsson[40] has claimed that only one (i.e. Geirröðr) of the two otherworld chiefs in Icelandic tradition is derived from Norse mythology whereas the other, Goðmundr á Glæsivöllum, has his origins in "Celtic" fairy tales (see *Þorsteins þáttr bæjarmagns*). J. Simpson[41] has elaborated on his likeness to Bran of Celtic tradition and argued that the horn of plenty, Grímr the Good in *Þorsteins þáttr bæjarmagns,* is derived from "stories about Bran's horn and severed head as talismans of plenty and protection."[42] Simpson thinks, however, that these motifs may have reached Iceland via continental romances.

In the most recent study of Icelandic otherworld journeys, Rosemary Power[43] has argued that even though continental works "may have reinforced the use of the otherworld theme, the analogues to the Norse secular tales are to be found in Irish secular works, which were written in Irish and did not enjoy widespread circulation."[44] She therefore claims that the more likely route for these motifs to Iceland was "in oral form during the period of settlement in the late eighth and ninth centuries."[45]

39 Ed. in *Flateyjarbók* I, 29-36.
40 (1959) 18.
41 (1963), esp. 512-13.
42 J. Simpson (1966) 19.
43 (1985).
44 R. Power (1985) 167.
45 Ibid, 156. For another fairly recent discussion of the topic, see M. Ciklamini (1968).

59

Saxo has a story of a voyage of Gorm and Thorkel to Goðmundr á Glæsivöllum[46] which resembles *The Voyage of Bran*.
They know that it would be fatal to taste the fruits or enjoy the
women of the Ódáinsakr if they want to return. "In the event,
those who actually succumb lose their wits. The supernatural
world of Guðmundr is fatal to those who do not resist its
charms."[47]
Hadding, a prehistoric Danish king, is reported in Saxo to
have undertaken a journey to the underworld, escorted by a
woman,[48] a journey of a similar nature to the Adventures of
Connla and Bran in Ireland.[49]
The Welsh story of *Pwyll Prince of Dyfed*,[50] can be taken as a
possible literary source for a passage in the Icelandic *Egils saga
ok Ásmundar*. Both are concerned with encounters between
people of the two worlds and even though they contain common
folk motifs, the motifs appear "as an elaborate part of a complicated story"[51] and should therefore be regarded as an example
of a borrowing.

In both a living prince is out hunting and overtaken by night, and loses his
companions. At dawn he has an encounter with a supernatural being, in both
stories called Arawn (Arán), with whom he makes a strange compact to spend a
stated period of time in the supernatural regions, the details of which vary
according to the variation between Norse and Welsh pictorial representation of
the abode of the dead. In both stories a combat takes place in the abode of the
dead between the living man and a dead one, though again there is a slight
variation here because the Welsh story has introduced a second king of this
abode. In both stories the living man succeeds in dealing a mortal wound to his
dead (supernatural) adversary, and in subsequently making his way out of the
world of the dead to his own home and his own people.[52]

46 J. Olrik (1925) I-II, 435ff.
47 N.K. Chadwick (1957) 197.
48 J. Olrik (1925) I-II, 93-94.
49 N.K. Chadwick (1957) 197.
50 In *The Mabinogion*, 3-24
51 N.K. Chadwick (1957) 173.
52 Ibid, 175-76.

There are two distinctive elements which suggest strongly that these stories must be linked in some way. First, that the combat is preceded by a hunting scene in which the hunter is lost and secondly that the otherwise unknown name, Arawn (Arán) occurs in both stories. The Icelandic form, Arán, suggests an oral connection because it represents the pronunciation of the Welsh form. Chadwick suggests, from a passage in *Landnámabók*[53] concerning a certain Ásmundr whose father settled on the Hebrides, that the story originated in the Hebrides and spread from there to both Iceland and Wales. In the episode in *Landnámabók*, Ásmundr's slave is buried with him and later rescued. The episode therefore gives us a glimpse into otherworld beliefs.

Further, love-affairs between members of the two worlds can be mentioned. The fairy mistress is common in Gaelic tradition and elsewhere, an example of which may be found in *Serglige Con Culainn* where Cú Chulainn becomes a lover of the fairy, Fann, who had wasted away through love for him. In Iceland the motif is most common in the FAS where "the supernatural lady is sometimes the hero's foster-mother, and sometimes his mistress, and on occasions she is both (cf. the Irish tale of Scáthach)."[54]

5.2.1.4. *Álfar, Huldufólk and Síd-folk*

This brings us to Icelandic beliefs in relation to *álfar* and *huldufólk*. Here things are even more obscure and uncertain

53 *Hauksbók*, see *Landnámabók* 105. It is also of interest to note that Ásmundr's former wife, Þóra, is said to have built a guest house (p.105) right across the high road. J. Young (1937) 118-19, has suggested that this should be connected with Irish *bruiden*.

54 Einar Ólafur Sveinsson (1959) 17, who believes the model for the Icelandic stories to be "Celtic tales which found their way to Iceland at a very early time." ("the Irish tale of Scáthach" is in *do Fogluim Chonculainn*, see p. 63).

than elsewhere. Einar Ólafur Sveinsson has claimed that Irish and Icelandic fairies are "much more poetically-minded than Norwegian fairies",[55] whatever that may mean. The general nature of Icelandic *huldufólk* and Irish *síd-folk* also shows similarities which supposedly reflect Irish influence on Icelandic.[56] The influence is seen as having reached Iceland with immigrants from the British Isles.[57]

5.2.1.5. Voyages to the West

Both Irish and Icelandic traditions have preserved stories about voyages to the west. In Ireland, these stories are marked with vivid imagination, whereas the Icelandic ones appear to be more realistic — which is not surprising since Viking settlement has actally been found in North America.

T.J. Westropp[58] has compared these tales. He leaves it open which influenced which but has no doubts that bearers of both traditions knew of each others' tales. But even so:

> The features in common of the Norse sagas and Irish *imrama* are few — the vines in Vinland, the wooded and grassy shores, and the attack of the dark-skinned natives, the "wonder strands," the sea full of maggots which attack Bjarne's hide-boats, and the adventures with whales are the chief.[59]

Westropp then proceeds to compare Irish tales of the legendary islands in the Atlantic with classical ideas about Atlantis,

---

55 (1959) 21

56 Detailed research appears to be lacking in this field. Einar Ólafur Sveinsson (1940) 156, and later (1975) esp. 108-12, has compared Menglöð in *Fjölsvinnsmál* to Welsh and continental literatures without, it seems, any definite conclusions. In his earlier work (p.157) he also referred to usage of bright colours and the Everlasting battle as something derived from 'Celtic' material but all this remains very unclear.

57 Einar Ólafur Sveinsson (1940) esp. 156-57. Also H.F. Feilberg (1910) who looks at the nature of elves in Scandinavian and Irish traditions.

58 (1913).

59 T.J. Westropp (1913) 235-36.

how they spread and how these islands appear on maps. It is of course clear that similar stories about wonderlands far away are not exclusive to Ireland and Iceland. It would nevertheless be interesting to examine the possibility of the two countries having something in common in these respects which might make them distinctive from the rest of the world. It can for example be considered that if Icelandic tales about Vínland owe their origins to Irish *imrama* as well as real expeditions, it must be in such a way that those who found North America or told the stories of these expeditions, identified the newly found land with the wonderlands of the Irish. Hence a tentative explanation of the obscure name, Vínland. It is considered very unlikely that vines grew in the areas found by Vikings in America but if the stories have this double background, the name Vínland is easily understandable.[60]

5.2.1.6. *Supernatural Fosterages*

Finally, supernatural fosterages must be mentioned. As a young man, the Norwegian king, Haraldr hárfagri, follows a certain Finn[61] or Dofri[62] into a supernatural fosterage where he remains for five years. This echoes an Irish story in which Cúldub is pursued by Finn macCumaill to a *síd* because he stole some food from Finn.[63]

This story of Harold would seem to relate that the king received supernatural fosterage, that he received a cup of mead from the beautiful daughter of his fosterer, that her father promises him the sovereignty on his departure, and that he marries the lady, who has alternatively beautiful and also hideous and

60 J. Young (1937) 120ff, has a discussion on these possible double origins and how "Hvítramannaland" (White Men's Land), thought to be west of Ireland, was identified with the lands in the west, discovered by Icelanders and now known as America.

61 According to *Hálfdanar saga svarta*, ch. 8.

62 According to *Flateyjarbók* I, 564-66.

63 In *Finn and the Man in the Tree*.

baleful aspects. The close relationship of these supernatural experiences of Harold to those of the Irish High-King Conn Cétchathach, and still more to those of Conn's descendant, Niall Noígiallach, and their relations with the maiden calling herself the *flaithiusa h-Erenn* ("the Sovereignty of Ireland") requires no demonstration.[64]

Hilda R. Ellis[65] has given an account of instances of fosterings by giants, and described ideas on the nature of giants in Old-Icelandic literature. Her account is a useful summary of the Icelandic material but she only suggests that this might be similar to what is found in "Celtic" tradition. As an example, she mentions the story of Cú Chulainn and his fostering by Scáthach and his temporary "marriage" with her daughter, Uathach (in *do Fogluim Chonculainn*).

It forms a close parallel to the tales of the giant fostermothers in the *Fornaldar Sögur*, and indicates clearly that it will be necessary in pursuing the subject further, to enter fully into the difficult question of Celtic influence in Norse literature, or perhaps it would be wiser to say the interrelationship between the literature of the Scandinavian and Celtic worlds.[66]

The general resemblances that have been pointed out here are not by any means conclusive proofs of literary borrowings. What they show, however, is that certain aspects of the ideology in the two cultures under discussion are closely related. One must also bear in mind that if most of the influence from the Gaelic world came to Iceland before the year 1000 and was of a similar nature and significance as outlined above then it is hopeless from the very start to expect to find anything which might suffice as proof in these matters. What is most likely to be found, as in the instances above, are similar features in underlying beliefs and attitudes. These could have survived for the

64 N.K. Chadwick (1957) 191-92. She also maintains that the appearance of a Finn in the Icelandic version is significant (192). *Bárðar saga Snæfellsáss* is also of great interest with regard to supernatural fosterage.

65 (1941).

66 H.R. Ellis (1941) 85.

64

two, three or even four hundred years during which the stories would have been told and reshaped in Iceland. Binding evidence is not available, and never will be, in this field. But the most likely development can be suggested from the existing evidence, taking into account the wider historical context and other features which suggest literary links.

5.2.2. Single Motifs

5.2.2.1. Starkaðr and Cú Chulainn

Starkaðr in Old Norse tradition[67] has been claimed to be akin to the Irish Cú Chulainn.

A. Olrik[68] pointed out a literary parallel, between an episode in Saxo Grammaticus[69] where Starkaðr sits naked in the snow and looks for lice in his clothes, and the Irish *Táin Bó Cúailnge* where Cú Chulainn finds himself in a similar situation.[70] A. Olrik considers the Irish story to be the original.[71]

It seems, however, that the opposite may equally well hold true. Even though "exposing oneself to rough weather"[72] can be found in Irish hagiographical works, this says but little about this particular motif as it appears here in *The Táin*.

In *The Táin*, Cú Chulainn's sitting naked in the snow, looking for lice in his shirt does not have the same deep-rooted function

67 For references to Starkaðr (mainly in FAS and Saxo Grammaticus), see M. Ciklamini (1971).
68 (1910) 66-67.
69 J. Olrik (1925) vol I-II, 313-14 (before a battle with Angantýr and his brothers).
70 Recension I, II 1255ff.
71 See also Einar Ólafur Sveinsson (1959) 13; J. Milroy (1977) 127; P. Hermann (1922) 449-54; A.G. van Hamel (1933) 275-83, who compares what he calls "weather magic" in the two cultures. It is interesting to note that in *Vatnsdœla saga*, a spell formula for weather magic is said to be in the Irish language (ch.47). Ketill Hængr also sits in the snow when preparing for a battle (see his saga).
72 A.G. van Hamel (1933) 276.

in the story as in the case of Starkaðr. In fact it seems to be thrown in without any connections with what happens before or after. Starkaðr is preparing for a battle and the snow storm may have magic origins.

The hero enters into relation with the blind elementary powers themselves. He flings a challenge at them, sustains their violence ungrudgingly, and thus wrings the magical power from them, which he requires for his next exploit.[73]

In spite of this difference in function, some connection is more than likely. But it is questionable whether A. Olrik's statements need be true, when he says that *The Táin* is older than the Starkaðr-story (as a written work this is of course true) and that the Cú Chulainn's episode in question "passer godt in".[74]

Apart from this single motif, the passive aspect of Starkaðr's heroism is believed to be of similar nature to what can be found in descriptions of Cú Chulainn's endurance of wounds. Rather than to describe the heroes' activity and ability to inflict wounds and death upon others, what is emphasized is their ability to endure wounds.[75]

Starkaðr also refuses to have his wounds dressed until a peasant's son who is an acceptable healer because he earns his living by honest toil, comes along. Starkaðr's refusal is paralleled in *The Táin*. Cethern mac Fintain returns severely wounded from a battle and refuses all treatment except what will enable him to go on fighting for three days and three nights, after which he collapses and dies.[76] In both traditions

73 A.G. van Hamel (1933) 280.

74 A. Olrik (1910) 67 ("fits in well").

75 *Táin Bó Cúalnge — from the Book of Leinster*, ll 3145ff and 3230ff — scenes from the battle between Cú Chulainn and Fer Diad. J. Olrik (1925) 314ff (after the battle with Angantýr — see above). J. Milroy (1977) 127, says about Starkaðr's capacity to endure discomfort and wounds, that it puts him "in a different world from the more restrained sufferings of classical heroes (Odysseus, for example), and is most like the Irish."

76 *From the Book of Leinster*, ll 3626ff, where the wounds receive very detailed attention - - to say the least.

... the motif of the wounds and their relief exemplifies the warrior's endurance and magnifies his fortitude, but the literary treatment is different. Whereas the Irish story is pushed to a fantastic and humorous extreme apparently for its own sake, the tending of Starkaðr's wounds is made into a little allegory of the social order.[77]

Further, it might be of interest to consider the supernatural circumstances of Starkaðr's birth. Some of these may have parallels in Irish tradition.

The single motif in the Starkaðr story, however, seems to be still another example of general resemblance rather than a direct borrowing.

5.2.2.2. Injuries in Dream

Å. Lagerholm [78] drew attention to a parallel between the Irish story, *Serglige Con Culainn*[79] and the 14th century *Ála flekks saga*,[80] "which also contains other Celtic motifs."[81]

The relevant passages tell of how Cú Chulainn and Áli are whipped in their sleep and left seriously ill. Here the Icelandic saga is regarded as the receiver.[82] It may also be noted that before Cú Chulainn falls asleep, he throws a spear at two birds flying with a gold chain between them. This motif does not occur in *Ála flekks saga* but has been claimed to appear in Saxo Grammaticus.[83]

77 J. Milroy (1977) 128-29.

78 (1927) LXV-LXVI.

79 The relevant passages are respectively from ll 71 (par. 8) and pp. 179 onwards in T.P. Cross and C. H. Slover (1969).

80 Ed. by Å. Lagerholm (1927). See esp. pp. 105ff (ch.12).

81 Einar Ólafur Sveinsson (1959) 17, who is referring to álög-motifs, spell-formulas and werewolf-motifs (see below).

82 In addition to the above, see also M. Schlauch (1934) 136; Einar Ólafur Sveinsson (1975) 47.

83 A. Olrik (1910) 290-91; P. Hermann (1922) 403; J. Olrik (1925) vol. I-II, 289. The passage in Saxo tells of how Fridlev, son of Frode, hears and sees

5.2.2.3. Werewolves and Álög — Spells

Belief in werewolves is common in Europe and is sometimes associated with the motif of the unfaithful wife who changes her husband into a wolf. Some scholars think that this was originally "a Celtic story or a Celtic version of a story which is known elsewhere."[84] The motif is known in Iceland, e.g. in Ála flekks saga, which "in details große übereinstimmungen mit der keltischen Werewolfs Tale zeigt."[85]

The origins, however, of the motif in Iceland are not clear: "... it is probably derived from continental medieval sources, although it is possible that there existed in Iceland old werewolf stories of Celtic origin."[86]

The origins of werewolf stories must be seen in the light of closely linked stories, namely those associated with álög, or spells. The idea of spells is of course extremely common and is most often concerned with a human who is changed into an animal, a monster, or a troll.

In Icelandic tradition, however, we come across a special type of álög which is."very little known in Scandinavia."[87] In these the hero has to carry out a feat, losing all peace of mind until the mission is completed. Einar Ólafur Sveinsson wants to connect

three swans in the air the night before his battle with Aamund. The swans drop a belt which A. Olrik and P. Hermann think to be of a similar nature to the chain in Irish. Saxo, however, does not say clearly that the birds are tied together with the belt. To explain this, both Olrik and Hermann claim that the motif has been borrowed without an understanding of its mythical significance. The present writer would welcome a comprehensive study of that significance!

84 Einar Ólafur Sveinsson (1959) 10.

85 Å. Lagerholm (1927) LXIV ("agrees in great details with the Celtic werewolf tale"). For further references of instances in Iceland, see Einar Ólafur Sveinsson (1959) 11.

86 Einar Ólafur Sveinsson (1959) 11.

87 Ibid, 19. See there for further references.

this type with a certain aspect of the Irish *geis*[88] where the spell-bound party is forced to perform certain tasks.[89]

In a thorough study, Einar Ólafur Sveinsson[90] has investigated the nature of *álög* in the Eddaic poems, *Grógaldur* and *Fjölsvinnsmál* and *Hjálmþérs saga,* and shown that they are of the same type as those in the Welsh story of *Culhwch and Olwen*[91].

In these tales a stepmother lays a spell on the young prince that he shall have no peace of mind until he finds a certain princess. When the princess has been found the prince has to accomplish some feats. In an earlier work, Einar Ólafur Sveinsson[92] had concluded that the Icelandic stories differed too much from the Welsh version to make it likely that they were derived directly from Welsh tradition. He therefore suggested a common ancestor, which, however, he was unable to specify. Later[93] he claimed to have found this "missing link" in the Irish story of Art mac Con (*Echtra Airt meic Cuind*) where the stepmother's spell is preceded by a game of *fidchell* as in the Icelandic *Grógaldur* and also in the Danish ballad *Ungen Svejdal* where the spells are preceded by a game of some sort.[94]

A certain counter spell-formula is also likely to have come into Icelandic tradition from the Irish, since it does not seem to

88 J.R. Reinhard (1933) esp. 299ff.

89 J.R. Reinhard (1933) 301, 305 and R. Thurneysen (1921) 470 for Old Irish examples.

90 (1975) 13-116.

91 In *The Mabinogion* 95-136. H. Falk (1893), (1894), thought that they were all influenced by medieval Graal-stories but Einar Ólafur Sveinsson (1975) 25 has shown that this is very unlikely since the Icelandic stories in question do not contain any of the main motifs of the Graal-legends — most importantly, no Graal.

92 (1959) 20.

93 (1975) 75.

94 Einar Ólafur Sveinsson (1975) 75 thinks that the Danish ballad was influenced by Icelandic poems.

appear in Scandinavia.[95] In both traditions a female character
lays a spell on the male hero, who in turn puts a spell on the
female that she may stand with each foot on some raised features in the landscape (towers, hills, cliffs), feeling miserable
until the hero either dies, gets rid of the spell or comes back.
Thereupon the female offers to lift the spell but the male
refuses. Apparently there is little doubt that the counter-spell
formulas have reached Iceland from Ireland and in his most
recent conclusions, Einar Ólafur Sveinsson still holds to what
he earlier wrote:

The Icelandic dialogue is an old oral translation from the Gaelic one, and I
assume that this translation took place in Iceland.[96]

In this connection we may also observe what Einar Ólafur
Sveinsson calls the "Loathly Damsel motif,"[97] which is for
example found in the Irish *Echtra mac Echach*. Here we are told
of how Niall of the Nine Hostages meets an old hag beside a
fountain. The hag promises to give him water if he kisses her.
This he does and she is immediately transformed into a lovely
young lady who introduces herself as the "Sovereignty of Ireland."

This motif is widespread in Irish, English and continental
sources alike, of which Einar Ólafur Sveinsson mentions two
further examples: The English ballad *The Marriage of Sir
Gawain* and Chaucer's *Wife of Bath's Tale* in *The Canterbury
Tales*.[98]

In Iceland the motif frequently appears in the FAS and later
in modern folktales. Its almost total absence in Scandinavia,
however, would suggest that it did not reach Iceland from the

95 See Einar Ólafur Sveinsson (1959) 22-24; (1975) 76ff.
96 (1959) 23.
97 Ibid, 19.
98 (1959) 19.

continent but rather that "the origin of these Icelandic stories was in the British Isles."[99]

5.2.2.4. The Beheading Game

Einar Ólafur Sveinsson[100] has investigated the beheading game in the Icelandic *Sveins rímur Múkssonar* and in the Irish story *Fled Bricrend* where Cú Roi is beheaded three times, only to recover instantly. In the *rímur* a certain Grámann arrives at court and invites those present to cut off his head, if he can in return, cut their heads off the following day! Similar stories are found in French and English sources but no single one of them can be regarded as the source for the Icelandic version.[101] The Irish story is closest to the Icelandic one but influence from Arthurian works indicates that the *rímur* could not have derived their material directly from Irish tradition. A now lost source, possibly written in England might therefore have served as an intermediary.[102]

Further examples of a similar nature could be offered, almost ad infinitum. But what has been pointed out here should suffice to show what sort of influence one can expect to find in the FAS material. Before proceding to the mythology, however, it should be of interest to draw attention to a recent study by N. Lukman of *Sörla þáttr* and related material.

5.2.2.5. Irish Substratum in Some Fornaldarsögur

N. Lukman[103] has discussed several FAS, *Sörla þáttr eða*

99 Ibid.
100 (1975) 119ff.
101 Einar Ólafur Sveinsson (1975) 134.
102 The uncertainty in Einar Ólafur Sveinsson's conclusions shows, if nothing else, very clearly how complicated these studies are bound to be and how little we can often end up with after a long day's journey into the wilderness of motif-origins. This can be borne in mind elsewhere in the present work where conclusions often seem quite definite and straightforward.
103 (1977).

Héðins saga ok Högna, Sörla saga sterka, and *Hálfdanar saga Brönufóstra* and compared them with material from Irish sources which tell of events in Ireland during the second half of the ninth century.[104] He argues that the Icelandic accounts depend on a written Irish source, similar to the Frg. The present writer, however, cannot see how an oral connection can be ruled out. What is interesting in this comparison is that Ireland is never mentioned in the Icelandic texts. If they have used the Frg. as a source, it is in such a way that conflicts taking place in Ireland have been transferred to a Scandinavian setting but the names of the Scandinavian leaders have been preserved. What points to the Irish source in particular is the name Sörli and his association with monasticism which is paralleled by the Irish Suairlech, abbot of Clonard (died 870).

Lukman also traces:

Nordic distortions of Irish names and words: e.g. Finn — finnskr, Fyn; Gall — galdr, Gellir; Luimnigh — ljómi; mná — Mána; Brenann — Brana; Maelsechlainn — Molda and Sleggja; scrín — Skrímnir; leit-rí — (Latinised) Litidorum. One Irish-sounding name is found in the saga, Karmon, the name of Sörli's teacher.[105]

Finally Lukman presents us with a fascinating note on numerology. In *Sörla þáttr* we are told a version of the story of Hjaðningavíg which differs from that found in other Scandinavian sources. It is fought on the island Há ("Iona (Ir. Hí; Ia, Annals of Clonmacnoise: Hugh)"[106]) and it continues for 143 years when it is brought to an end by Ólafr Tryggvason, king of Norway, and Ívar ljómi. By correcting the chronology in *Snorra-Edda,* which also tells of the Hjaðningavíg, Lukman is able to identify Ólafr Tryggvason with Ólafr kvaran Sigtryggsson, king of Dublin, who left the city in 980, totally

---

104 Here he is referring mainly to *Annals of Ireland. Three Fragments copied from Ancient Sources.* (Frg.) as well as other Irish annals.
105 N. Lukman (1977) 56.
106 Ibid, 57.

72

defeated, and died on a pilgrimage in Iona the year after. He similarly identifies Ívar ljómi with Ivar Luimnigh whose reign in Limerick was brought to an end by the Irish in 977-8. These two events were interpreted by Irish chroniclers as the end of an epoch marked by Viking tyranny. And this is where the Hjaðningavíg in *Sörla þáttr* can be compared with the Irish sources: The battle lasted 143 years as well as the Viking tyranny in Ireland, " — a calculation made from the annals, where the first viking's name to be entered, Saxolbh, is s.a. 837. Add 143 years to that and we are in 980, the year Óláfr kvaran left Dublin for Iona."[107]!

Leaving aside these calculations, we can still look at the way Irish material is changed and transformed and taken out of Ireland. It is hard to imagine why the sagas (i.e. if they were created by Scandinavians for Scandinavians) could not be set in Ireland with the Norsemen fighting fiercly against the Irish. But if they came from a similar mould as is suggested here for the FAS, — with people of Gaelic origins telling stories to their Norwegian/Icelandic masters in Iceland — these would be the changes and adaptions most likely to occur; perhaps even with an underlying and well hidden vein of anti-Viking propaganda.

107 Ibid, 57.

Chapter VI

MYTHOLOGY

6.1. *Scandinavian Background*

Old Norse/Icelandic mythology as it has been preserved, mainly in *Snorra-Edda* and the Eddaic poems, mostly written in Iceland in the 13th century, has its origins, at least partly, in pagan times. It can be assumed that the general framework of ideas concerning the gods was brought to Iceland as it existed at the time of the settlement. The ties with Scandinavia never broke so that myths which were later attached to Scandinavian gods could travel back and forth and be told on both sides of the Atlantic, in Iceland and Scandinavia alike. But these were scattered stories and linked up with poems about the gods. Knowledge of these, however, was fundamental for scaldic poets and their audience in order to understand kennings and the poetic vocabulary, much of which is based on the mythology.

The status of the gods was established by the Scandinavians themselves, who composed|poems and told stories about them.

The Gaels who were faced with this tradition in Iceland could not have affected its roots or its general background. It is another matter how faithfully our sources reflect Old Norse mythology and pagan beliefs, or how much influence Christianity had on the tradition during the centuries. Such questions need not concern us here. Because of the nature of the material in pagan times, lack of an authoritative collection of myths related to the gods and a lack of any institution which decided on what was genuine tradition and what was not, the stories were open to additions and variations. New stories could be told about the gods and fitted into what had been told of them before. It is in this manner that the Gaelic material could become a part of Old Norse/Icelandic mythology without changing its basic assumptions.

One may therefore suggest that Gaelic influence in Old Icelandic myths would be likely to be limited to single motifs and episodes, a few of which will now be discussed.

6.2. Single Gaelic motifs

6.2.1. The Sons of Tuireann and Loki

From Ireland comes a story, called *The Fate of the Children of Tuireann* (see esp. pp. 188-89 and 196-97). The text dates from the 18th century but references to its contents are found as early as in *The Book of Leinster* (1160)[1] and A.B. Rooth[2] has argued that it might reflect an even older story.

The sons of Tuireann get the task of fetching the apples of life. They fly off as hawks, take the apples but are pursued by fire-vomiting ladies in the form of griffins. The sons — as hawks — catch fire, change again into swans, dart down into the sea and complete their mission.

In *Haustlǫng* (a poem dated to the 9th century) and *Snorra-Edda* we find a story of how Loki saves his life from the giant Þjazi (who is in the form of an eagle) by promising to bring him Iðunn and her apples of youth. This he does and when the Æsir find out they send Loki off to fetch them back. Loki transforms himself into a hawk, fulfils his task but is pursued by Þjazi, again in eagle guise, into Ásgarður. There, at the right moment, the gods light a fire into which Þjazi flies and is killed.

S. Bugge[3] has claimed that the Irish story depends on classical

1 See E. O'Curry (1862) 394-97.
2 (1961) 20.
3 (1889).

sources (this is deduced from the number of tasks involved, similar to those of Hercules, and the occurence of the name "Hisbe" which supposedly goes back to Latin "Hesperus/Hisperus") whereas *Haustlǫng* and *Snorra-Edda* are derived from the Irish.

In a more recent study, A.B. Rooth has accepted Bugge's argument, saying that:

The tale of the sons of Turen agrees with regard to the order of motifs and details with the myth of Þjazi, for example the chasing in eagle guise; griffins chase hawks (the sons of Turen); fire, breathed out by the griffins, singes the hawks so that they fall into the sea; [...] it would seem that the motif of the burned hawks has been transformed into the motif of Þjazi burned by the fire of the Ása gods.[4]

Rooth further argues that apart from this the author of *Haustlǫng* was acquainted with material from the British Isles as well as classical authors. She concludes, however, that the apples did not come into the poem from classical authors directly, but "probably through an intermediary British source such as the tale of the Sons of Turen."[5]

This story, however, would need to be subjected to more detailed research, and further comparison with other areas must be made before any final conclusions can be drawn.

6.2.2. *Táin Bó Fraích and Þórr's Visit to Geirröðr*

The Irish story *Táin Bó Fraích* has been suggested as a source for Þórr's visit to Geirröðr (in *Þórsdrápa* and *Snorra-Edda*, Skáldskaparmál, ch. 27)[6]

In *Táin Bó Fraích* the king, Ailill, lures Fróech to swim in a pool in which, he tells him, he knows of no danger. Fróech has to take off his belt and swims without a weapon, across the pond

4 A.B. Rooth (1961) 19. See 18-21 for her discussion.
5 Ibid, 21.
6 A.B. Rooth (1961) 72-75.

to fetch a branch of rowan. He is attacked by a water-monster which clings to him. Fróech receives a sword from Ailill's daughter, Findabair, whereupon Ailill throws a spear at Fróech which he catches in the air and throws back. He misses Ailill but the spear goes through his mantle and shirt. Then Fróech kills the monster with the sword, gets out of the pool and is taken away by a host of otherworld women to recover.

Loki lures Þórr to go to Geirröðr and tells him that the road is without dangers so Þórr leaves without his weapons but accompanied by Loki/or Þjálfi. Þórr obtains a magic belt, staff and iron gloves from a certain Gríðr with whom they stay overnight. On the way they have to pass a river and Þórr uses the staff from Gríðr to support himself, wading through the water with Loki/ Þjálfi clinging to his belt. The river starts to rise and looking around him, Þórr sees the cause of this sudden rise: a giantess (or two, Geirröðr's daughters) standing with her legs spread, further up and producing large quantities óf liquid. Þórr then grabs a stone and throws it at her, saying that a river should be stemmed at its mouth. Climbing out of the river he seizes a rowan tree for support. Þórr continues to the otherworld where Geirröðr resides and kills his daughters with the staff. Geirröðr throws a glowing metal lump/bar at Þórr which he catches with the gloves from Gríðr and throws back at Geirröðr. The bar goes first through a pillar, then through Geirröðr and finally through the wall, and into the ground.

Rooth has drawn attention to the following parallels[7]: 1) The monster clings on to Fróech "in the same way as Þjálfi (Loki) hung on to Þórr."(72) 2) Þórr and Fróech are both fooled into leaving their weapons behind them. 3) The river in Þórr's story is parallelled by the pond in Táin Bó Fraích. 4) The rowan tree appears in both stories but with a different function. 5) They receive a weapon (staff/sword) from a woman. 6) They both catch a spear/iron bar which is thrown at them and send it back.

Fróech's cast is harmless but Þórr, who never misses, does not miss this time either.

Rooth concludes that these parallels are "too numerous and too peculiar to be explained as "natural" in their contexts or as spontaneously originated parallel phenomena."[8] And since *Táin Bó Fraích* appears to be older than our oldest Icelandic source (*Þórsdrápa*) the receiver is deemed to be the Icelandic/ Scandinavian tradition.

6.2.3. Death of Fergus — Death of Baldr

Similar conclusions are drawn in Rooth's work with regard to the relationship between the Old Irish *Aided Fergusa* and the story of Baldr's death, mainly found in *Snorra-Edda* (Gylfaginning, ch. 33-35, but references to it are also in *Völuspá, Baldrs draumar,* and Saxo).[9]

In *Aided Fergusa,* Ailill gets the blind fosterbrother of Fergus, Lugaid, to throw a spear at Fergus where he is playing joyfully with Medb, Ailill's wife, in a lake. Ailill tells Lugaid that these are a hart and a doe in the lake. Another version in *Silva Gadelica*[10] tells of how Ael (Ailill) kills Ferchis (Fergus) by throwing a spear of "hardened holly" at him, pretending to be aiming at a stag.

In *Snorra-Edda,* Loki fools Baldr's blind brother, Hǫðr, into throwing a sprig of mistletoe at him and thus join in a favourite entertainment of the gods, namely, throwing objects at Baldr. This was a harmless game since all things had sworn to spare Baldr — except the mistletoe which was considered "too young" to swear. The mistletoe proves fatal and Baldr dies.'

Comparing the Baldr myth with classical, Christian and Oriental motifs, Rooth concludes that these are too different

8 Ibid, 73.
9 See A.B. Rooth (1961) 110-114.
10 P. 119 and p. 129 in translation.

from the Scandinavian version which agrees in details with traditions from the British Isles. "This indicates that the Baldr myth [Parts 1-2] has come to Scandinavia direct from, or has been influenced by the tradition in, the British Isles."[11]

The dialogue between Loki and Hǫðr is parallelled by the dialogue between Ailill and Lugaid. In the Irish however, Lugaid's blindness is essential "whereas in the Scandinavian tradition it gives the impression of having been clumsily combined with the *mistletoe* as the only effective weapon."[12] It may also be noted that the motif of a plant in this connection is known in Ireland. The idea of a blind figure involuntarily killing his fosterbrother/brother is of course the same.

These examples from Rooth's study will suffice to show the nature of the relationship as argued for by her. Surprisingly, Rooth does not compare Bricriu, the troublemaker in Irish tradition, with his counterpart in the north, Loki. Turville-Petre[13] discussed this resemblance, referring to Dumézil, and claimed that Bricriu bore "a distinct resemblance to Loki"[14] without elaborating on that likeness in any detail.

6.2.4. *The Masterbuilder*

C.W. von Sydow has tried to establish a connection between stories in the Irish Finn cycle about a masterbuilder and *Snorra-Edda* (Gylfaginning, ch.25) where a giant builds Ásgarðr for the gods with the assistance of his horse, Svaðilfari. A similar story is also told about a certain Finn (according to von Sydow the name itself suggests a connection with the Irish) who builds the cathedral in Trondhjem. The story has spread in Scandinavia and been attached to other church buildings.[15].

11 A.B. Rooth (1961) 110.
12 Ibid, 113.
13 (1964) 145.
14 Ibid.
15 C.W. von Sydow (1907) (1908); and (1920) 26-27.

This motif is widespread in the Finn-cycle. The masterbuilder offers to take on a project with his horse and complete it within a certain period. In *Snorra-Edda* the builder asks for Freyja as a reward as well as the sun and the moon. The last mentioned objects are used by von Sydow as an indication that the story originated in Ireland. He feels that this is too much to ask for as a reward and besides, it is not within the gods' power to give the sun and moon away. This, he claims, could be based on a misunderstanding of an Irish idiom:

"do-bheirim grian agus éasga", ordgrant översatt: "jag ger sol och måne", men dess verkliga betydelse är: "jag svär vid sol och måne" eller helt enkelt: "Jag försäkrar dyrt och heligt". Det ligger nära till hands att en sådan formel skall missförstås av en person som ej är förtrogen med iriskans alla egendomliga idiom, översättas ordgrant och uppfattas som ett lönevillkor, i stället för vad det är, en bekräftelseformel. Men då är det också tydligt at det är nordborna som här varit låntagare.[16]

The problem has been discussed by numerous scholars, some of whom have held views irreconcilable to that of von Sydow. The motif is widespread in Scandinavia and whether its origins lie in Ireland or not is of no vital importance for the present discussion. If it is Irish, it may have reached Scandinavia relatively late, possibly via the Orkneys (see p. 47). Its popularity, though, might be seen as an argument against such late foreign influence.[17]

16 Ibid (1920) 27. (""do-bheirim grian agus éasga", literally translated: "I give sun and moon", but its real meaning is: "I swear by sun and moon" or simply: "I declare by everything I hold dear and holy." It is easy to see how such a formulaic expression could be misunderstood by a person who was not familiar with all the local idioms of the Irish language, and then translated literally and regarded as a promise of reward, instead of what it is, a formula of assurance. If so, it is also clear that it is the Norsemen who have been the borrowers.").

17 Apart from von Sydow's articles, see for example W. Liungman (1942); M. Fossenias (1943); I.M. Boberg (1955). M. Chesnutt commented on this whole discussion, saying: "It must be said, in justice to von Sydow, that none of his critics have accounted satisfactorily for the form of the Irish variants." ((1968) 126fn. See there for further references).

6.2.5. Þórr's Visit to Útgarða-Loki

A much more detailed study was carried out by von Sydow[18] on Þórr's visit to Útgarða-Loki (in *Snorra-Edda*, Gylfaginning ch. 26-31) in which he argued for Irish origins of the story. He was later criticized by Finnur Jónsson[19] which led to lively debate on this particular story, methodology and the Irish question in general in *Folkminnen och Folktankar* the year after.[20] This debate shows, among other things, how entirely correct von Sydow was when he earlier wrote in 1920:

A andra sidan verkar än i dag blotta misstanken om lån från kelterna på germanisterna som ett rödt kläde på en tjur. Knappast någon germanist har underkastat sig mödan att lära sig det utomordentlig svåra gaeliska språket, och kännedomen om keltisk tradition har sålunda ej kunnat framtvinga en undersökning om sammanhanget.[21]

Ever since, scholars have been expressing their respective opinions on the possible Irish origins of Þórr's visit, most recently R. Power,[22] where references to earlier works may be found.

All this effort, however, has not led us to the ultimate goal, i.e. to prove beyond doubt where the story originated. Power's conclusions still leave us with questions to be answered even though it is hardly reasonable to call for more detailed research than that which has already gone into this particular story.

18 (1910).
19 (1921) 104-13.
20 C.W. von Sydow (1922); Finnur Jónsson (1922).
21 P. 22 ("On the other hand, the mere suspicion of a borrowing from the Celts affects the Germanists as a red rag affects a bull. Hardly any Germanist has undertaken the task of learning the extremely difficult Gaelic language, and a knowledge of Celtic tradition has thus not been able to promote an investigation of the connection.").
22 (1985*).

Although it remains a possibility that 'Þórr's Visit' is independent of the Irish tale, the similarities are so great as to suggest some connection. In the absence of any evidence of a common source it is reasonable to assume that this is one case in which an Irish tale reached Iceland.[23]

We are always faced with the same results. We have to judge for ourselves which is the most likely interpretation of the evidence, basing our judgement on what can be learned from other sources. Individual elements tell us but little until they have been accumulated and thus give support to each other.

6.2.6. Talking Heads

Talking Heads appear in Old Icelandic sources, the most famous example of which is Mímir's head, which Óðinn prevents from rotting by smearing it with herbs. The head then speaks to him, tells of various tidings and hidden matters.[24]

A. Ross[25] has looked at the nature of severed heads in Celtic cultures. Of particular interest to us in this connection is the association of heads with wells. Ross[26] discusses this aspect of the beliefs and points out the similarities with Mímir's head and well. Óðinn's herbal treatment, she says, is "in the manner of the Celts, who preserved the heads of their enemies with oil and herbs"[27] and further:

23 R. Power (1985*) 260-61.
24 *Ynglinga saga*, chs. 4, 7. References to Mímir's head are in *Snorra-Edda* (Gylfaginning ch.38), *Völuspá*, st. 46 and *Sigrdrífumál*, st. 13. Apart from this, talking heads in Old Icelandic material are to be found in *Eyrbyggja saga*, ch. 43 and *Þorsteins þáttr bæjarmagns*, ch. 9 (see p. 58). Severed heads of enemies appear in *Orkneyinga saga*, ch. 5 (see pp. 45-6), *Grettis saga*, ch. 82, *Bjarnar saga Hítdælakappa*, ch. 32, *Fóstbræðra saga*, ch. 18, and *Ljósvetninga saga*, (Þórarins þáttr). Finally, supernatural qualities are attached to heads in *Ólafs saga Tryggvasonar*, ch. 28/19, *Eyrbyggja saga*, ch. 27, and *Njáls saga*, ch. 157 (i.e. the head of King Brjánn). See also Þorvaldur Friðriksson (1985).
25 (1959) (1962); see also her book (1967) 61-126.
26 (1962).
27 Ibid, 41.

Thus we have, in a Norse context, a group of motifs which, untypical as they are of Norse tradition, are completely familiar from Celtic sources. The decapitation of the head, its preservation, its association with a well, and its powers of prophecy and otherworlds knowledge are all features which recur in Celtic tradition and belief. All the evidence suggests that this episode in Norse mythology, if not a direct borrowing from a Celtic source, at least owes its presence in the Norse tradition to a detailed knowlege on the part of the story-teller of such beliefs amongst the Celts.[28]

Elaborating on this possibility, J. Simpson[29] has considered the myth of Mímir with the idea in mind that he was essentially the Head and can be traced to "Celtic" material. Thus "Celtic" origins for this belief can explain what in Icelandic sources alone appears to be confusing and contradictory.

6.2.7. Rígsþula

Irish influence on Rígsþula seems to be well established and generally accepted.[30] The poem tells of the origins of three classes in society. Rígr (identified with Heimdallr in a prose introduction to the poem) travels from one married couple to another and sleeps with the woman in each place he visits, thus begetting the forefathers of slaves, free workmen ("karla ættir") and earls. A favourite problem of Old Norse philologists, the age of the poem, will not be dealt with here. Both the early 10th and the 13th centuries have been suggested. What concerns us is, first, the name of the poem. The Ríg- is taken to be derived from the Old Irish genitive singular, ríg of rí, meaning king.

Einar Ólafur Sveinsson[31] has summarized several parallels between the poem and Irish material. He compares the god Rígr with the Irish Dagda who is called Ollathaer — "the great

28 Ibid, 41.
29 (1965).
30 Einar Ólafur Sveinsson (1962) 251-53, 287-91.
31 (1962) esp. 252-53.

father" — and begets a son, Mac Óc[32] ("young boy", similar to Konr ungr ("ungr" means "young") in *Rígsþula*) on another man's wife. The custom that a noble visitor is entitled to sleep with his host's wife is known from Ireland but not in Scandinavia.[33] Konr ungr also masters some power over birds which reminds us of Cú Chulainn[34] and his son, Conlae.[35]

Rígsþula is unique among the Eddaic poems in its realistic and detailed descriptions of domestic matters and different classes. In this it resembles an Old Irish law text where similarly detailed descriptions of different social orders, their possessions, dress and eating habits, may be found.[36]

Einar Ólafur Sveinsson thinks that the poem was probably composed in the tenth century by a person who was familiar with the British Isles.

32 This is Óengus in *Aislinge Óenguso*.
33 See J.I. Young (1933) 102 and references there.
34 In *The Táin* Recension I, l 781ff. Also in *Serglige Con Culainn*.
35 In *Aided Óenfir Aífe*.
36 Apart from Einar Ólafur Sveinsson, see J.I. Young (1933) 100-01, who says: "In its minute description of the appearance, dress and food characteristics of the three classes of society *Rígsþula* exhibits Irish affinities." (100) Young also draws attention to the description of Mother in *Rígsþula* where "the poet heightens his description and employs synonymous adjectives in a typically Irish manner." (101) In *Rígsþula*, st. 28-29, the description of Mother reads: "hugði at ǫrmum, / strauk of ripti, sterti ermar. // Keisti falld, / kinga var a bringu, / siðar slæður, / serk blafaan; / brun biartari, / briost liosara, / hals hvitari / hreinni miǫllu." ("The lady sat, at her arms she looked, / She smoothed the cloth, and fitted the sleeves; / Gay was her cap, on her breast were clasps, / Broad was her train, of blue was her gown, / Her brows were bright, her breast was shining, / Whiter her neck than new-fallen snow." Transl. by H.A. Bellows (1968) 210-11 (st. 28)). This, she says, may be compared with a description in *The Táin* (Recension I, ll 32-37) of Feidelm, the poetess of Connact: "Agad fochóel forlethan. Dí broí duba dorchaidi. Abrait duib dáin co mbentáis foscod i mmedón a dá grúaide. [...] Teóra trillsi fuirri .i. dí thriliss immo cend súas, trilis tara haiss síar co mbenad a dá colphta inna díaid." ("Her eyebrows were dark and black. Her beautiful black eyelashes cast a shadow on to the middle of her cheeks. [...] She had three plaits of hair: two plaits wound around her head, the third hanging down her back, touching her calves behind.").

In her study of *Rígsþula*, Young[37] drew attention to Heimdallr's popularity in the British Isles as is reflected on sculptured crosses with images identified as Heimdallr. She then proceeded to show affinities between a tale in the *Rennes Dindšenchas* (p. 294-95), explaining the river name Inber n-Ailbine, and references to Heimdallr in *Völuspá in skamma* (st. 7) and in the lost *Heimdallargaldr*, quotations from which are preserved in *Snorra-Edda* (Gylfaginning, ch. 15 and Skáldskaparmál, ch. 16).

In both the central figure is a son born of nine mothers and in both there is an allusion to the use of a human head as a missile. The resemblance becomes the more striking when we remember that *Völuspá in skamma* states that Heimdall's mothers were sea maidens and that he was nourished on the ice cold sea. The only serious discrepancy between the Heimdall myth and the legend preserved in the *Rennes Dinnsenchas* is that in the former case the offspring of the nine mothers is slain by a head used as a missile whereas in the latter this same person's own head is used as a weapon. This latter legend however recalls Snorri's kenning for a sword, — Heimdall's head.[38]

Young suggests that the poem may have been composed around the year 1000 and is a result of contacts in the British Isles between Scandinavians and Gaels; contacts which allowed for friendly cultural exchange by that time.

N.K. Chadwick[39] compared Manannán mac Lír, who is associated with the Hebrides and the Isle of Man, and Heimdallr, and pointed out similarities in their association with the sea, shape changing and their function as begetters of children. From this she postulated that the Hebrides were "the centre of distribution of the whole mythological and literary nucleus"[40] connected with these two figures.

There is no apparent reason why one should doubt the presence of Gaelic elements in *Rígsþula*, elements which can

37 (1933) 102ff.
38 Ibid, 104-05.
39 (1955) 111-15.
40 Ibid, 115.

explain why the poem is different from other Old Icelandic poetry. But as the commentators have argued, the poem represents an example of later cultural contacts. It has had no radical, deep-felt influence in Iceland on the mythological tradition as a whole and can therefore hardly be a product of the "melting pot" there.

The general conclusions which may be drawn from looking at Gaelic influence in Old Norse/Icelandic mythology are therefore in line with what was said earlier. It neither formed the tradition nor changed its basic characteristics.

Chapter VII

THE ICELANDIC FAMILY SAGAS

The Icelandic Family Sagas have been an endless source of discussions and theories about their origins. It has been claimed on the one hand that they are entirely created by the writer with nothing but books to work with and on the other that they are fairly accurate reproductions of oral sagas. The development of saga writing is not within the scope of the present work; the native tradition behind them is.

7.1. *Local Influence on Individual Sagas*

The Family Sagas derive their subject matter mainly from events within Iceland from the time of settlement onwards. How these events were eventually transformed into written prose literature in the 13th century is a subject for another study. The native tradition which created the mould for saga writing owed its origins, according to the present hypothesis, to the Gaels who settled in Iceland. By the time, however, that some sort of oral native sagas would have developed, the Gaels had been assimilated into the population and the "Gaelic originals" of stories which had been brought to the country were therefore, by then, also forgotten.[1]

Gaelic elements in the Sagas seem to confirm this assumption. Sagas which come from the west of Iceland (e.g. *Laxdæla*

---

1 At least some time had to elapse between the events and a saga about them. What such "sagas" were like, in details, nobody knows. Here it is nevertheless taken for granted that the information was passed down, orally, open to change and by no means stable and fixed.

saga and *Kjalnesinga saga*) where Gaels or people from the Gaelic world were among the named settlers, show more signs of Gaelic influence than others. This could perhaps be explained by the presence of a stronger Gaelic element in these areas than elsewhere, thus allowing for a more deep-felt influence than we come across in other sagas.

7.2. Laxdæla Saga

Laxdæla saga comes from Dalasýsla in the west of Iceland where the principal settler was Auðr/Unnr djúpúðga, said to have been married to Ólafr hvíti, king of Dublin. She left Dublin sometime after his death and arrived in Iceland towards the end of the 9th century via the Scottish Isles. She was a Christian (see p. 19).

One of the characters in the saga, Hǫskuldr, buys himself a slave-woman (Melkorka (Ir.) Mael-Corcrae[2]) in Norway. She turns out to be the daughter of Mýrkjartan ((Ir.) Muircertach), called king of Ireland. She speaks Irish and teaches that language, secretly, to her son Ólafr pá (Hǫskuldsson). Ólafr travels to Ireland to refresh the family ties and returns to Iceland as a glorious travelled man. In Iceland he marries the daughter of Egill Skallagrímsson (she complains about Ólafr's slave origins but falls for his charm when they meet). Their son is Kjartan (named after his Irish grandfather), the main male hero of the saga and believed to show some Irish characteristics.

Given this background, *Laxdæla saga* should, more than any other saga, bear traces of Irish influence. And indeed it does even though the results are no more certain in this case than elsewhere.

Einar Ólafur Sveinsson[3] has compared the Irish episodes in *Laxdæla saga* with Irish historical sources and claims that as far as it goes it does not contradict what we know from Ireland.

2 Hermann Pálsson (1964) 396.
3 (1934) LX-LXXII.

Hermann Pálsson[4] has compared Kjartan and St. Cellach in the Irish saga *Caithréim Cellaig*, written about 1200 but based on older material. St. Cellach lived in the sixth century. The main similarities lie in their religious habits and their death. They both observe Lent so that news thereof spread around and they are killed just after Easter. They become famous for their devotion and are loved by all — with a few exceptions! They are both killed by their cousins and fosterbrothers. A dream predicting their deaths is dreamt on Wednesday. Their deaths by weapons have also been prophesised earlier. The killers in both cases are fooled or incited to kill these lovable characters who also share a certain scepticism when they are invited to their enemies.[5]

Hermann Pálsson does not conclude much from these parallels but says that they show how doubtful all conclusions in these matters are bound to be.

Further parallels were pointed out by G. Turville-Petre[6] and N.K. Chadwick[7] who mentioned the red-eared white horses which Bolli offers to his fosterbrother, Kjartan. These are believed to link up with similar horses in the *Táin Bó Fraích*, "and also from Welsh stories, both secular and ecclesiastical."[8]

Helgi Guðmundsson[9] has discussed these points. Even though such coloured horses are rare in Icelandic literature, they do occur and Helgi Guðmundsson thinks that knowledge of them could have reached Iceland via other routes than from the British Isles.

It seems, however, that the most likely and the simplest

4 (1964).

5 See Hermann Pálsson (1964) esp. 401-02. For an English summary, see Magnus Magnusson and Hermann Pálsson (1969) esp. 36ff.

6 (1953) 248.

7 (1957) 171-72.

8 N.K. Chadwick (1957) 172. It may be of interest to note that white red-eared cows do exist in the British Isles (O. Bergin (1946) and J. Bell (1985)).

9 (1967) 101-02.

explanation for a saga such as *Laxdæla saga* is that this horse
motif originates in Ireland and was preserved orally in Iceland.

Again in ch. 63 of this same Icelandic saga [i.e. *Laxdæla saga*] occurs the motif,
extremely common in Irish literature (e.g. *The Intoxication of the Ulstermen,
Bricriu's Feast, Da Derga's Hostel,* and the *Cattle Raid of Cualnge*), in which a
hero or king or queen, when about to be attacked, orders one of his faithful
servants (Bolli orders his shepherd in the *Laxdale saga*; Queen Medb orders
her prophetess Fedelm in the *Cattle-Raid*) to enumerate the approaching foe,
attaching to each a brief description by which the person to be attacked
recognises everyone of his foes and names them by name. [...] This motif is
common in Irish; but in Norse it seems to occur only here, where other Irish
elements are also prominent.[10]

Laxdæla saga is generally regarded as being quite distinctive
among the Icelandic sagas. It uses more colours, pays more
attention to details in appearance etc. than other sagas. The
saga has been interpreted as reflecting medieval romances in
these matters.[11] These and other characteristics of the saga
have also been thought to be feminine[12] and a female author
has even been suggested.[13] Such observations are of course far
too general to allow us to conclude much from them. But it
could perhaps be that these characteristics are due to an unusu-
ally strong Irish influence in the district which fostered the saga.
The influence need not only be guessed at from motifs in the
saga but statements to that effect can also be read in the saga
itself. The settler in the area is a Christian from Dublin, but of
Norwegian origin and one of the characters learns Irish secretly
from his slave mother, visits his mother's country, Ireland, etc.

10 N.K. Chadwick (1957) 172. See also G. Turville-Petre (1953) 248-49.
For a treatment of this in Irish, see J. Carney (1955) 305-21. Another description of the approaching enemies which are identified can also be found in Ólafs
saga Tryggvasonar in *Heimskringla* I, ch. 101, where Eiríkr jarl identifies the
ships of Ólafr Tryggvason's navy. There, however, Eiríkr sees the ships himself.
   11 See for this: Einar Ólafur Sveinsson (1934) § 1.
   12 Ibid, VI, XIff.
   13 Helga Kress (1980).

Melkorka is worthy of special attention. The only reason why she is acceptable as a mother for an Icelandic hero, is that she is in fact a princess. Nevertheless, her son has to suffer in Iceland for his ignoble mother! If this was the case with royal persons from Ireland who were captured into slavery, how much more so for slaves of less noble status. Can we expect them to be mentioned at all?

7.3. Kjalnesinga Saga

Kjalnesinga saga comes from a district where people of Gaelic origin are said to have settled. Helgi Guðmundsson[14] has pointed out an interesting parallel between the Boyhood Deeds of Cú Chulainn[15] and an episode in *Kjalnesinga saga* (ch. 7-8).

At the age of five, Cú Chulainn leaves his mother for the first time and goes to her brother, King Conchobar (*Kjalnesinga saga* (ch. 1 and 2) has a reference to Konofogor (Conchobar), King of the Irish) in Emain Machae, and plays with his play-spear and other toys on the way. Among other things he throws the spear ahead of him and then runs after it to catch it before it lands. When he arrives he is attacked by the three-times fifty lads in Emain Machae but fights them off successfully and is protected by Conchobar.

In *Kjalnesinga saga* a certain Kolfiðr leaves his mother for the first time and goes to a playing field. On the way he plays with a stick which he throws ahead of him and runs after it. We are not told whether he catches it in the air (he might even be using it to jump across rivers. This is not clear from the text). Later he uses his wooden-stick as a weapon, when he kills a certain Qrn. After that, Kolfiðr is protected by his mother's brother, Korpúlfr. Korpúlfr is otherwise unknown.

14 (1967) 92-93.
15 *Táin Bó Cúailnge*, Recension I, ll 399-456.

Helgi Guðmundsson seems to recognize these parallels but he does not analyse them in any conclusive fashion. The main point of comparison, however, concerns the father-son battle motif which both Cú Chulainn (in *Aided Óenfir Aífe*) and Búi (nicknamed "hundr", meaning dog), the main hero of *Kjalnesinga saga* (ch. 18) take part in.

Both Búi (ch. 13-14) and Cú Chulainn (*do Fogluim Chonculainn* 134-37) beget sons on their travels with otherworld ladies overseas. The sons later come to their fathers. When the sons arrive, Cú Chulainn believes that this might be his son, Búi, on the contrary, does not believe his son when he introduces himself. In both stories, father and son fight each other but neither of them can win. In the Irish tale, Cú Chulainn finally uses a special weapon obtained from the sister of his son's mother, and in *Kjalnesinga saga* the outcome is the reverse. Búi falls, accusing the boy's mother of some supernatural intervention in their fight.

M. Schlauch[16] investigated these episodes and compared them with continental stories of a similar kind. She considered the Irish and Icelandic variants to display special similarities which suggested a connection between them. Einar Ólafur Sveinsson,[17] who continued the discussion, belived *Kjalnesinga saga* to be an echo of Irish tales about Cú Chulainn, brought to Iceland by the settlers on Kjalarnes. He also emphasised the occurrence of the name Konofogor, the fact that Búi is called *hundr* (Cú Chulainn means Dog of Culann) and that "he is the only one of Icelandic champions who is armed with a sling."[18]

Helgi Guðmundsson[19] has later discussed all these and finds possible sources in various Icelandic and Norwegian books, both translations and original works, for the name Konofogor,

16 (1934) 114-18.
17 (1959) 15.
18 Ibid. Both Cú Chulainn and his son use a sling. See *Táin Bó Cúailnge* Recension I, ll 680, 766; and *Aided Óenfir Áife*.
19 (1967) 83-94.

Búi's nickname "hundr", and the sling. He claims that it is simpler to explain their origins from these works rather than from stories of "Celtic" origin[20]. The father-son combat is discussed at some length but the only conclusion drawn is that it is difficult to ascertain the origins.[21]

Finally, Helgi Guðmundsson points out that the story, if it is derived from the Irish, must have been brought to Iceland during the Settlement period and later developed within the country and continues:

En um þetta verður ekkert fullyrt. Sé sögnin í rauninni keltnesk og vestrænt landnám á Kjalarnesi staðreynd, er þó vafasamt, að hún hafi geymzt staðbundin þar alla tíð frá landnámsöld fram undir 1300.[22]

The only reason why it should be doubtful that the story was preserved in the area is the occurrence of the name Kolumba in the saga and Kólumkilli which was what Icelandic and Irish laymen used to call St. Columba (Colum Cille). This observation, deriving from Hermann Pálsson, is referred to in Helgi Guðmundsson's work.[23] Hermann Pálsson argued that this showed the importance of written sources as opposed to oral. But as Helgi Guðmundsson points out himself[24] then it is likely that the learned version of the name became increasingly popular in writing due to influence from the church. This point, therefore, proves nothing about the oral origins of the story.

Opposing the point that it is unlikely that stories were preserved it may equally well be said that it was very likely that Irish stories were preserved. The present writer sees no reason

20 Ibid, see p. 94.

21 Ibid, see p. 92.

22 Ibid, 94 ("But about this nothing can be asserted. If the story is really Celtic and western settlement on Kjalarnes a fact, it is nevertheless doubtful, that it was preserved locally all the time from the Age of Settlement until 1300.").

23 Ibid, 84-85.

24 Ibid, 110-13.

why this should be unlikely, especially in an area where some of the settlers are recorded as Gaelic and Christian.

With regard to Helgi Guðmundsson's statement that it is simpler to point to written sources it seems that such explanations are much more complicated than simply saying that these features are among those which are likely to have circulated orally in Iceland among people with Gaelic ancestors and can therefore easily find their way into a saga which is based on their lore.

Finally we may note that if we were faced with the task of finding an Icelandic name, equivalent to the Irish Cú, it is doubtful that we could come up with a more suitable name than Búi hundr. Búi contains the same vowel as Cú and "hundr" is a translation of Cú![25]

7.4. Bandamanna Saga

Another more dubious parallel is mentioned by N.K. Chadwick[26] between flytings in Scéla Mucce Meic Dathó and Bandamanna saga. In Scéla Mucce Meic Dathó, the Connachtman, Cet mac Mágach insults seven Ulster heroes in a mannjafnaðr, basically accusing them of being worse warriors than himself and showing signs of injuries they have received from Cet. This is done in order to decide on the best hero among them. The winner is entitled to carve the pig which is being served.

In Bandamanna saga (ch. 10), a company of 8 confederates disintegrates because of a law-suit. This is caused by two of them, Egill and Gellir, who separate themselves for their own

---

25 According to Kjalnesinga saga Búi dies at the age of 27 (Helgi Guð-mundsson (1967) 10). Helgi Guðmundsson notes (ibid, 93fn. 4) that this is the same age as J. Carney ((1955) 279) postulates for Cú Chulainn's death. This parallel, he says, is doubtless a coincidence.

26 (1957) 172.

advantage. Egill, in justifying their decision, has a row with four of his former confederates, accusing them of being unreliable, mean about food or generally ludicrous. In one case only, is there a mention of some physical injuries suffered by the insulted person. In the Irish story these play an important role. The only point of similarity (excluding, however, that there is a group of eight in both cases) is that when a person has been defeated in this verbal battle, he sits down. Apart from the fact that there is not much to do for a person who has stood up to argue with someone and lost the argument except to sit down again, the usage of the phrase is quite different in the two stories. In the Irish it is formulaic (used in six cases out of seven) and marks the end of each episode. "Dessid side dano" ("thereupon he sat down") is used five times and "Téit Óengus ina suide" ("Óengus goes to his seat" or "in his sitting (position)") is used once.

In *Bandamanna saga* the characters are standing upright after listening to Gellir's judgement which Egill has the task of publicly justifying. One person only is sitting down, Þórarinn, who appears to have difficulties in standing on his feet because of his great obesity. When he tries to stand up to argue against Egill, Egill immediately orders him to sit down — which he does and listens to the insults from his seat. The phrase used is: "Hann settisk niðr" ("He sat down"). In another manuscript[27] however, Þórarinn stands up without any comment on how fat and heavy he is, listens to Egill and sits down afterwards, "sezk niðr ok þagnar" ("sits down and falls silent").

There is therefore no obvious connection between these two episodes. In Iceland some sort of flyting, *mannjafnaðr*, was common enough, both in literature and, presumably, in real life. Egill himself refers to this practice used for entertainment:

---

27 Both texts are printed in the same edition on the same page, one on top of the other.

Þess betr þykki mér, er þú lastar mik meir ok þú finnr fleiri sonnur á því, ok af því at mér var þat sagt, at þér hofðuð þat fyrir olteiti, at þér tókuð yðr jafnaðarmenn, ok tóktu mik til jafnaðarmanns þér.[28]

7.5. Bárðar Saga Snæfellsáss and Eyrbyggja Saga

Both *Bárðar saga Snæfellsáss* and *Eyrbyggja saga* which come from the west of Iceland, show certain affinities with Gaelic material in their love for the supernatural. *Bárðar saga* has already been mentioned in connection with supernatural foserage (p. 63) and *Eyrbyggja* in relation to magic heads (p. 81). Further, Einar Ólafur Sveinsson has noted that the Fróðárundur (Fróðá wonders) in *Eyrbyggja saga* are "associated with a woman from the Hebrides, and they include several elements which look out of place in the history of Icelandic folklore."[29] In the absence of a more detailed study of these sagas with regard to Gaelic influence, these general observations will have to suffice.

7.6. Kormáks Saga

It has been mentioned that *Kormáks saga* shows general "Celtic" characteristics, esp. in the verses. "[...] there is an impetuosity, a fire, a passion in his [i.e. Kormákr's] verse that assimilates it much more closely to the literature of the country of his paternal descent [i.e. Ireland] than to the colder, more restrained poetry of the North."[30] It has been more difficult to point out exactly which passages in the saga have Irish parallels.

28 P. 354 (Möðruvallabók). "The more you find fault with me and justify your insults, the better I like it. That's because I've been told that you and your men used to amuse yourselves over drink by comparing yourselves to others, and now you've chosen me as your equal." (Transl. by Hermann Pálsson (1975) 83-84).
29 Einar Ólafur Sveinsson (1959) 14.
30 E. Hull (1903) 261.

J. Carney[31] argued that the whole plot is derived from Irish stories of the Tristan type and mentions *Comracc Líadaine ocus Cuirithir* as the closest Irish version to *Kormáks saga.* Einar Ólafur Sveinsson[32] on the other hand has claimed that nothing could be more unlike the love of the Tristan type than Kor-´mákr's love.

Kormaks saga is a story of love that crumbles away, it is a "tragedy of frustration", and nothing could be less like it than Tristan; and yet both of them are love stories. But then love is one of the main subjects of the world's poetry, and by itself, of course, has nothing to tell us about literary relationship.[33]

But there are other minor points which draw our attention to Ireland. Kormákr's name is almost certainly Irish (Cormac). In the saga his grandfather is said to have been a Norwegian Kormákr but Einar Ólafur Sveinsson[34] has shown that the saga's genealogy is not in agreement with other more reliable sources. He therefore suggests on this name evidence that Kormákr "was to some extent of Irish origin."[35]

In one of Kormákr's verses, the word *díar* appears and Einar Ólafur Sveinsson[36] has claimed that this is derived from the Irish *día*, meaning god.

An episode in chapter 26 of the saga tells of eels which wind themselves around Kormákr. This motif could also have originated in Ireland.[37]

A fundamental problem in the case of *Kormáks saga*, con-

31 (1955) 225-28.
32 (1959) 15fn.; (1966) 58-59.
33 Ibid (1966) 59. An interesting point, mentioned by Carney ((1955) 228fn.) is that the first element of Liadan's name, "lia", can mean "stone". Similarily, the first element in the name of Kormákr's beloved, Steingerðr, also means "stone".
34 (1966) 26-28.
35 Ibid, 27-28.
36 (1975) 209.
37 Ibid, (1966) 57-58 (1975) 210 and references there to Irish examples and earlier observations.

cerns the age of the written work and its possible continental sources. Bjarni Einarsson[38] maintained that it was a purely fictitious work by a thirteenth century writer who used written sources for his subject matter and composed the poetry himself, again drawing on continental models. If this were the case, it would be futile to look in the saga for Irish material which had been preserved orally in Iceland.

Einar Ólafur Sveinsson[39] has pointed out that Bjarni Einarsson fails to show the actual link with the continental sources and says that there is no indication that the saga writer was an expert on scaldic poetry "and there are astonishingly many cases of contradiction between verse and prose — · i.e. he [i.e. the saga author] fails to understand them [i.e. the verses]."[40] Einar Ólafur Sveinsson[41] also maintains that the difference in style between the romantic poetry and the anything but romantic spirit of the prose suggests that the same person was not behind both.

Studying the linguistic evidence of the verses, he shows that many of them are likely to be genuine tenth century products, though by no means all.[42]

If Kormákr's poetry indeed dates from the tenth century and the legendary and/or historical Kormákr is in any way linked with Ireland, then he constitutes important evidence for the origins of scaldic metres (see p. 113).[43]

38 (1961).
39 (1966) 25.
40 Ibid, 38.
41 Ibid, 51-53.
42 Ibid, 28ff.
43 It may also be one of these numerous "accidental" parallels that a duel-scene in *Kormáks saga* between Kormákr and Hólmgǫngu-Bersi is so similar to a duel scene in *Kjalnesinga saga* between Kolfiðr and Búi that Helgi Guðmundsson has suggested a written connection with *Kjalnesinga saga* as the receiver ((1967) 57, also 16-18). Perhaps this similarity could be explained otherwise with some common background in mind.

98

7.7. Egils Saga

Bo Almqvist[44] has looked at what appears to be a proverb in
Egils saga, "Er konungsgarðr rúmr inngangs, en þrǫngr
brottfarar", ("The king's court is wide to enter, but narrow to
depart from") spoken by Arinbjǫrn in chapter 68, when he is
assisting his friend Egill to get hold of some money which rightly
belonged to Egill but had been seized by the king. Almqvist
shows that this is the only occurrence of this saying in Iceland
and it is rarely found in Scandinavia.[45] In Ireland, however, it is
widespread in modern tradition, which leads Almqvist to
suggest that this might have reached Iceland with settlers from
that area. Speculating on this possibility, he mentions references in the saga to "Dyflinnar skíði" (ch.4), visits to Dublin in
chapter 32 and 33, Irish slaves who belong to a settler in the
vicinity of Egill, called Ketill gufa and referred to in the saga
(ch. 77), Egill's half-Irish son-in-law, Ólafr pá, whom we know
from *Laxdæla saga,* and numerous references to Scotland and
the Scottish Isles in the saga.

Almqvist then discusses a famous episode in *Egils saga* (ch.
78) when Egill, upon his son's death, has decided to starve
himself to death. Egill's daughter, Þorgerðr — wife of Ólafr pá
— comes to him and claims that she wants to join him. After a
while she starts chewing seaweed, a custom which Egill seems
unfamiliar with, since he makes inquiries about the nature of
this "food", asking whether it is bad for you. "Very bad",
Þorgerðr says and Egill immediately asks for some! Eventually
he becomes thirsty from the salt and is then tricked into drinking milk, instead of water, thus spoiling his plan of fasting to
death.

Linguistic evidence from Iceland and The Faroe Islands
suggests that some of the vocabulary for edible seaweed is
derived from Gaelic and human consumption of seaweed also

44 (1966).
45 He mentions one similar example from Sweden (191-92).

appears to be limited to Iceland and the Faroes among the Nordic countries whereas it is well established in Ireland and Scotland.[46] In the light of this connection and Egill's unfamiliarity with edible seaweed, Almqvist asks:

Skulle, frågar man sig då, Þorgerðr ha lärt sig att äta tång av sin iriska svärmoder Melkorka eller sin make Óláfr pái?[47]

These hypothetical channels for Irish material into *Egils saga* can also be borne in mind in connection with a description of Egill in a foul mood and Cú Chulainn in his *ríastrad* or distortion linked with battle-fury. Jan de Vries[48] mentioned the similarity between these episodes but argued that Egill's *ríastrad* recalls Óðinn's image with only one eye and "can be explained entirely from North-Germanic tradition."[49] These passages, however, only echo each other with regard to the eyes; otherwise they differ in every respect. The Irish episode is a part of the Boyhood Deeds of Cú Chulainn and describes him just before he attacks the boys at Conchobar's court in Emain Machae:

Ríastartha immi-seom i sudiu. Indar lat ba tinnarcan asnort cach foltne ina chend lasa comérge conérracht. Indar lat bá hoíbell tened boí for cach óenfinnu de. Iadais indara súil dó conárbo lethiu indás cró snáithaiti. Asoilg alaile combo móir beólu midchúaich. Doérig dia glainíni co rici a hóu. Asoilg a beólu coa inairddriuch combo écna a inchróes. Atreacht in lúan láith assa mulluch.[50]

46 C. Matras (1958).

47 (1966) 188 ("One asks oneself whether Þorgerðr could have learned to eat seaweed from her Irish mother-in-law, Melkorka, or her husband Óláfr Peacock?").

48 (1963) 83-86.

49 Ibid, 84.

50 ("Thereupon he became distorted. His hair stood on end so that it seemed as if each separate hair on his head had been hammered into it. You would have thought that there was a spark of fire on each single hair. He closed one eye so that it was no wider than the eye of a needle; he opened the other until it was as large as the mouth of a mead-goblet. He laid bare from his jaw to his ear and opened his mouth rib-wide(?) so that his internal organs were visible. The champion's light rose above his head.") *Táin Bó Cúailnge*, Recension I, ll. 428-434.

The similarity with *Egils saga* is indeed small. The relevant passage describes Egill at King Aðalsteinn's residence after a victorious battle in which, however, Egill's brother, Þórólfr, had been killed. Egill comes to the celebration having buried his brother, sits down in silence and the only detailed description of Egill in the saga follows. Then we are told:

[...] en er hann sat, sem fyrr var ritat, þá hleypti hann annarri brúninni ofan á kinnina, en annarri upp í hárrœtr; Egill var svarteygr og skolbrúnn. Ekki vildi hann drekka, þó at honum væri borit, en ýmsum hleypði hann brúnunum ofan eða upp.[51]

The function of these two episodes is quite different. Cú Chulainn is preparing himself for attack, Egill is mourning his brother and is restored to his usual good humour only when he has received a gold ring from the king, starts drinking and composing poetry. When king Aðalsteinn further presents him with two chests of silver, he grows more cheerful: "tók Egill þaðan af at gleðjask".

We also observe that in *The Táin* the eyes are actually distorted whereas in *Egils saga* a more realistic method is used to create the same effect: Egill moves his eyebrows up and down.

Be that as it may, the evidence of the saga allows for Irish and Scottish material to have become mixed with stories about Egill even though it has left no definite mark on the saga.

7.8. *Njáls Saga*

Finally, an instance in *Njáls saga* should be mentioned. Apart from the account of the Battle of Clontarf which was referred to earlier (p. 47), there appears to be little Gaelic influence in the

51 Ch. 55 ("There he sat, just as we describe him, with one eyebrow sunk down right to the cheek and the other lifting up to the roots of the hair. His eyes were black and his eyebrows joined in the middle. He refused to touch a drink even though people were serving him, and did nothing but pull his eyebrows up and down, now this one, now the other."). Transl. by Hermann Pálsson and P. Edwards (1976).

saga. It is of interest, however, to note that the most outstanding and most celebrated of Old Icelandic heroes, Gunnar á Hlíðarenda, is presented with an Irish dog, Sámr, which Ólafr pá had brought back from Ireland.[52]

[...] hann [i.e. Sámr] er mikill ok eigi verri til fylgdar en rǫskr maðr. Þat fylgir ok, at hann hefir manns vit; hann mun ok geyja at hverjum manni, þeim er hann veit, at óvinr þinn er, en aldri at vinum þínum; sér hann ok á hverjum manni, hvárt honum er til þín vel eða illa; hann mun ok lífit á leggja at vera þér trúr. Þessi hundr heitir Sámr.[53]

This dog may not have a direct parallel in Irish sources but the fact that such a splendid dog is associated with Ireland calls to mind legendary dogs in Irish stories, with some of which the author of *Njáls saga* may have been familiar.[54] It is sufficient to mention the famous dog from the opening lines of *Scéla Mucce Meic Dathó:*

Boí rí amrae for Laignib, Mac Dathó a ainm. Boí cú occo. Imdíched in cú Laigniu huili. Ailbe ainm in chon, ocus ba lán Hériu dia airdircus in chon.[55]

The dog which Cú Chulainn first killed and then replaced in *The Táin*[56] is said to have come from Spain. That dog was held

52 Ch. 70. Ólafr was a half-brother of Gunnar's wife, Hallgerðr Hǫskuldsdóttir. This was mentioned by A. Olrik (1910) 291, as an example of "keltisk kultursammenhæng" ("Celtic culture contacts"). He also mentioned the dog Vígi which King Ólafr Tryggvason obtained in the west.
53 "He is a big animal, and will make as good a comrade-in-arms as a powerful man. He has human intelligence, and he will bark at every man he recognizes as your enemy, but never at your friends; he can tell from a man's face whether he means you well or not. He would lay down his life rather than fail you. His name is Sam." Transl. by Magnus Magnusson and Hermann Pálsson.
54 I do not know whether Irish dogs in reality were any better than dogs in general, whereas dogs in Irish stories were certainly quite extraordinary.
55 "There was a splendid king over Leinster, Mac Dathó [was] his name. He had a dog. The dog used to protect all Leinster. Ailbe [was] the name of the dog, and Ireland was full of the fame of the dog."
56 Recension I, ll. 542ff.

by chains during the day and let loose at night to guard his owner's grounds and protect his cattle. He, however, was not as intelligent as Sámr and attacked anything he was unfamiliar with, unable to "tell from a man's face whether he means you well or not"![57]

We see from these examples that Gaelic influence on the Icelandic Family Sagas is neither profound nor extensive. Sagas which come from districts where our historical sources and the Sagas themselves refer to settlers from Ireland or Scotland contain considerably more Gaelic elements than more "native" sagas, such as *Egils saga* and *Njáls saga*.

This need not be surprising since a stronger Gaelic element among the original settlers would probably have provided the mould for Gaelic stories to survive longer than elsewhere. In such conditions they could eventually become a part of local traditions instead of being limited to the oldest stories which were established already during the Age of Settlement, namely, the *Fornaldarsögur*.

The examples from *Egils saga* and *Njáls saga* show that the Gaelic elements in these are limited and can even be traced within the sagas themselves to the slave's son, Ólafr pá, the hero who gained recognition only because his slave-mother was of royal birth. He could therefore travel back to Ireland and renew the links with his mother's country. And the Irish influence through that man alone left its mark on the Sagas.

57 See for general information on dogs in Celtic traditions, A. Ross (1967) 339-41.

Chapter VIII

SCALDIC POETRY

8.1. Earliest Scalds and Evidence of Early Scaldic Poetry

Scaldic poetry was mostly practised by Icelandic poets. In Icelandic sources from the thirteenth century there are references to ninth century poets in Norway whose scaldic poetry has been preserved in these same sources. Bragi the Old is believed to have been the first to compose poetry in scaldic metre. There is some controversy as to his identity and he has even been identified with a god of poetry, also called Bragi[1] (*bragr* in Icelandic means a poem and poetic metres are called *bragarhættir*). If this Bragi can be placed among mortals he would most likely have been born around the year 830 and thus been an active poet in the second half of the ninth century.[2] From the nature of the sources it is hard to discuss with any certainty the actual identity of characters who are set so far back in time. Scaldic poetry is not preserved in Scandinavian runic inscriptions until about the year 1000 — and then in Sweden.[3] Recently discovered runes from Bergen in Norway show that scaldic poems were being composed there until the end of the thirteenth century, which is longer than previously thought.[4]

---

1 See G. Turville-Petre (1954) 47-51 (English translation (1972) 171-74) and references there to other works on the subject. Also same author (1976) xxi-xxiii.

2 Ibid, (1954) 49-50; (1972) 173; (1976) xxii. These conclusions are debateable.

3 Jakob Benediktsson (1983) 59 (under 'Dróttkvæði').

4 Ibid, 60 and 225 (under 'Rúnaristur').

Our sources mention two major Norwegian scaldic poets
from about 900, Þjóðólfr úr Hvini and Þorbjǫrn hornklofi, and
a third, Eyvindr skáldaspillir, who comes about half a century
later. Apart from these, most of the named scaldic poets came
from Iceland.[5] The first Icelandic poet to praise a king in his
poetry was Egill Skallagrímsson (born about 910). From the
second half of the tenth century onwards, we hear of maný more
Icelandic courtpoets and during the eleventh, twelfth and thirteenth centuries, Icelandic scalds are constantly employed at
the Norwegian court and sometimes also appearing at the
Swedish and Danish ones. Even the Earls in Orkney enter-
tained Icelandic scalds.[6]

We see from this that the evidence for scaldic poetry before
the settlement of Iceland is scanty and uncertain. It is not until
the first generation of Icelanders has grown up that our sources
can be relied on ·— and even then we have to be sceptical as was
mentioned above in the case of Kormákr (p. 97). Nevertheless
it is generally assumed that scaldic poetry first developed in
Norway.[7] If that was the case, it is hard to see why Icelandic
poets should have acquired what seems like a total and absolute
monopoly of the genre for centuries. What the sources tell us of
its origins has a mythical air and it is doubtful if much reliance
should be placed on them. To discuss the origins of scaldic
poetry in the light of the dubious character, Bragi the Old, and
use contradictory genealogies to assess whether he lived in the
first or second half of the ninth century, thus establishing the
starting point for scaldic poetry in the north, is as feasible as
calculating the age of mankind from Old Icelandic genealogies
going back to Óðinn.

The most concrete evidence relating to early scaldic poetry
are the Swedish runic inscriptions and the fact that in the late

5 In the twelfth and thirteenth centuries we know of two poets in the
Orkneys.
6 Jakob Benediktsson (1983) 59-60 (undir 'Dróttkvæði').
7 Ibid.

tenth century, professional scalds emerged in great numbers from Iceland and continued to do so during the succeeding centuries, making a living from their art all over Scandinavia and in the Norse colonies in the west. Scaldic poetry was also composed at a later stage in Norway as the runes from Bergen show. That activity, however, was not as professional as that of the Icelandic scalds.

Moreover, reference might be made to the observations of Barði Guðmundsson, [8] (see p. 28), that the vein of poetry appears to be stronger within certain families and that most of the named scalds came from the west and north of Iceland.[9] He also calls attention to the fact that more scalds than other people are known by matronymics, about 10% of scalds and 2% of others.[10]

If it is correct that scaldic poetry was practised as a distinctive art within certain families, it may indicate that some training was involved, and that scalds did not obtain their knowledge on mythology and metrics informally, but were instructed in these matters by some member of their family. *Snorra-Edda* certainly suggests that there were certain things which a scald should know to be properly qualified. It is impossible, however, to determine to what extent this was regarded as a special course of study.

In Ireland, on the other hand, we know that the *filid* were trained orally in special schools where they studied their art and

8 (1959) 109ff.

9 According to Barði Guðmundsson (ibid, 111), 13 court poets and 33 occasional poets came from the west, 13 and 28 respectively from the north, 8 and 15 from the south and only 1 and 8 from the east. Barði Guðmundsson uses this information, among other things, to argue that the Norwegian settlers who came to Iceland were of a separate race (the so-called 'Heruli') which had never integrated into the Norwegian population. The *herúlar*, as he calls them, are supposed to have used the opportunity when Iceland was discovered to move over there in order to practise their distinctive customs, among which was a special literary skill. This theory will not be discussed here.

10 Barði Guðmundsson (1959) 113.

received different degrees according to their stage of learning.[11]

Later, probably in the twelfth century, we come across "a number of literary families who dominated the profession of *filidheacht* and the related branches of *seanchas* 'history' and law throughout Ireland and who by precept and example maintained from one generation to another a stringent code of literary and linguistic practice."[12]

Whatever conclusions may be drawn from this, it seems that in both countries the art of poetry was looked upon as something which had to be consciously studied and developed in order to thrive.

On the above mentioned evidence alone, it would not be farfetched to suggest, with the historical background in mind, that scaldic activity in Iceland was the result of Gaelic influence.

8.2. *Scaldic Poetry — Eddaic Poetry*

Scaldic metres are different from what is known from Germanic poetry outside Iceland. Most of the Eddaic poems are composed in a metre, very similar to that of Old High German and Old English poetry, such as *Hildebrandslied* and *Beowulf*[13] There is no doubt that they have their roots in a common Scandinavian, and ultimately Germanic, tradition.

Eddaic poetry is anonymous, unlike scaldic poetry which is by known authors. The scaldic metres are elaborate and governed by strict rules, while the Eddaic metres are relatively simple and pliable, allowing for a style of diction which stands close to natural speech. Characteristic of scaldic poetry is also an intricate, not to say contrived, diction in which use is made of words not found in ordinary speech as well as elaborate cir-

11 See *Mittelirische Verslehren* and commentary by R. Thurneysen (1891) where the metres, the curriculum, and different grades of bards and *filid*, as described in the text, are discussed. See also P.A. Breatnach (1983).

12 P. Mac Cana (1974) 127.

13 G. Turville-Petre (1976) xii.

cumlocutions of the type called kennings. While such orna-
ments are not completely lacking in Eddaic poetry, they are
only occasionally found there. From the point of view of content, scaldic poetry deals mainly with contemporary happenings
and characters; praise-poems and commemorative poems are
two of the most common genres. The content of Eddaic poetry,
on the other hand, is almost equally divided between
mythological poems about Óðinn, Þórr and other ancient gods
and heroic poems, treating Sigurð the Dragon-slayer and other
Germanic heroes. They are thus set in mythical times or at least
far back in history.[14]

8.3. Scaldic Metres

What concerns us here and makes scaldic poetry so distinctive, are the metres and the syllable counting. "To be fully
scaldic, as I use the term, a poem must be in a syllable-counting
measure."[15] It is of great interest to note that two of the earliest
Norwegian scalds do not fulfil these requirements:

Many will disagree if I say that the scaldic poets were essentially syllable-coun-
ters; they will point to Þorbjǫrn Hornklofi's *Haraldskvæði (Hrafnsmál)* and
Eyvindr Skáldaspillir's *Hákonarmál*, saying that the authors of these did not
count their syllables. Poems such as those just mentioned have some of the
characteristics of scaldic poetry, those of subject rather than form, they could be
described as semi-scaldic.[16]

Scholars have noted that syllabic measures existed in Ireland
before the rise of scaldic poetry and a connection has therefore
often been suggested by some — and of course been rejected by
others.[17]

14 See for these general characteristics, Jakob Benediktsson (1983) 59; G.
Turville-Petre (1976) xi-xxi.
15 G. Turville-Petre (1976) xvii.
16 Ibid.
17 See G. Turville-Petre (1954); (1972) and references there to earlier
works.

It is not our purpose to go into any details in studying the Irish and scaldic metres but a limited survey of results with regard to their similarities will be offered.

8.3.1. Gabriel Turville-Petre's Studies

Gabriel Turville-Petre[18] discussed the problem of scaldic metres with regard to Irish influence after a long silence among scholars of Old Icelandic. He outlined the history of the Norsemen in Ireland, talked about the Gall-Ghaedhil (see p. 20), and about settlers in Iceland from the British Isles and argued for reasonably friendly cultural contacts as early as the ninth century thus leading to a mixed culture in Iceland from the very beginning. He then proceeded to give a survey of Irish metres and their Latin prototypes, compared these with scaldic metres and discussed the similarities and dissimilarities between the two. An account of Bragi the Old followed, in which Turville-Petre tried to determine when he could have lived (see p. 103), arguing that Bragi was the originator of the genre but also pointing to his connections with mythology. Turville-Petre believed that Bragi could have been in contact with Irish poets among the Gall-Ghaedhil and thus learned his art from them. He also finds some parallels in elaborate kennings in both Irish and Old Icelandic literatures.

Commenting on the general likelihood of Irish influence on scaldic metres he pointed out Irish influence on Scandinavian art and a rather dubious reference to an Irish poet entertaining the Scandinavians in Ireland. In conclusion he said that scaldic metres must have come into use in the late ninth century, probably under influence from "the sophisticated metres of the Irish filid."[19]

Finally he mentions the radical difference in subject matter, how "lyrical and delicate" the Irish poems are as opposed to the

18 Ibid.
19 Ibid, (1972) 177; (1954) 53.

"stiff and hard" Scandinavian poetry. As an exception from this, however, he quotes a stanza by Kormákr, dealing with love and nature. Let us look more closely at the features that are compared. Each line in the most popular Irish metre, *debide*, has seven syllables whereas in the most popular scaldic metre, *dróttkvætt*, it has six syllables.

> Inmain tír an tír út / thoir
> Alba cona / hingantaib:
> nocha ticfuinn eisdi-il / le
> mana tísainn le / Noíse.[20]

> Þél høggr stórt fyr stáli
> stafnkvígs á veg jafnan
> út med éla meitli
> andærr jǫtunn vandar...[21]

The important thing is the fact that the number of syllables is fixed:

[...] this difference [i.e. between the 6 and 7 syllables] is hardly of importance and may well owe its origin to poetic taste and the nature of the two languages. The Irish metre *Rinnard*, which is not at all unknown, consists of six-syllable lines which always end in a trochaic disyllable, just as do the lines of the *dróttkvætt* metre, for example:

> An clog sin ro / ghonais
> notchurfi-si ar / cráobhaibh
> gurbat aon re / hénaibh,
> an clog náomh re / náomhaibh.[22]

The number of stressed syllables can vary from line to line in Irish poetry whereas in scaldic poetry these are usually fixed, most commonly with three stressed syllables in each line. There

20 Ibid, (1954) 40; (1972) 163.
21 Ibid, (1954) 42; (1972) 165.
22 Ibid, (1972) 168-69; (1954) 45-46.

110

is, however, great controversy about stress in scaldic poetry and that cannot be dealt with here.[23] In both countries internal rhyme (*aðalhending/comhardadh slán*) and consonance (*skothending/uaithne*) are used. In scaldic poetry, *aðalhending* consists both of an identical vowel and the following identical consonants:

stafnkvígs á veg jafnan (*stafn/jafn*)

In Irish *comhardadh slán* only the vowels have to be identical and the consonants simply need to belong to the same consonantal group. The usage of this is different from scaldic metres where the *aðalhending* is within the same line. In Irish it appears most commonly as end-rhyme.[24] In the following example the endings of the second and fourth lines rhyme together and here the consonants are in fact identical.

Imdhe broc ag dol fa-a /dhíon
ann is miol muighe nach / mall,
is édan rionntanach /róin
ag techt on muir moir an / all.[25]

Similarily the scaldic *skothending* which is comparable to the Irish *uaithne*, differs from the Irish "in so far as the consonants must be identical, whereas in *uaithne* they need only belong to the same consonantal group."[26] ("þél høggr stórt fyr stáli" (Pél/stáli) and the final words of the first and third lines (dhíon/ róin) in the example above.)

A variety of metres are used by poets of both traditions. "One variation which the scalds used was to shorten or truncate alternate lines by removing the unaccented final syllable, so that the rhythm is completely changed."[27]

23 See ibid, (1954) 46-47; (1972) 169-70.
24 Ibid, (1954) 42-43; (1972) 165-66.
25 Ibid, (1954) 43; (1972) 166.
26 Ibid, (1972) 166; (1954) 43.
27 Ibid, (1972) 166; (1954) 43.

Fold verr folk-Baldr,
fár má konungr svá,
ǫrn reifir Áleifr,
es framr Svía gramr.[28]

A similar trick is found in Irish, in the so-called *debide gairit*
(the short debide):

Do chath / rod,
a Dhé nime, ni ma /lott,
ba Suibhne Geilt m'ainm iar/sin,
mh'aonar dhamh a mbarr / eidhin.[29]

Scaldic poetry, unlike Eddaic poetry, is strictly stanzaic with
eight lines in each stanza which is divided into two halves of four
lines each. These halves form a metrical and syntactical unit and
can be regarded as a basic unit of scaldic poetry. Similarly, the
Irish poetry in question is stanzaic with four lines in each
stanza.[30]

Some difference occurs in the usage of alliteration. In the
Irish it is used as an ornament whereas in scaldic poetry alliteration follows very strict rules. This is not surprising because
here the scaldic poets follow the pattern of alliteration already
well established in earlier Germanic poetry.[31]

End-rhyme is a point of difference as well. This can be fairly
elaborate in Irish poetry but is hardly known in scaldic poetry
except as a later development.[32]

In a more recent work on scaldic poetry, Turville-Petre[33] has
somewhat modified his views. He leaves the question of Bragi
the Old more open, drawing attention to his mythological

28 Ibid, (1954) 44; (1972) 167.
29 Ibid. For a further discussion on this point, see Einar Ólafur Sveinsson
(1975) 171-217; (1976). See below.
30 G. Turville-Petre (1954) 41; (1972) 164.
31 Ibid, (1954) 45; (1972) 168.
32 Ibid.
33 (1976) xxiv-xxviii.

background and emphasises the difference between the Irish
and scaldic metres, especially with regard to rhythm as was
mentioned above. In his conclusions, however, he still holds the
opinion that independent development is very unlikely:

Thus it seems that the strict rules governing the syllable count and the cadence
are the only significant features shared in common by Irish and scaldic poetry.
These rules are foreign to the traditional Germanic system, and it is hard to
believe that they developed among the two north-westerly nations independently.[34]

8.3.2. Einar Ólafur Sveinsson's Studies

In the meantime a study by Einar Ólafur Sveinsson[35] appeared in which he established that the prototype for *hnepptir
hættir*, catalectic measures, is most likely to be found in Irish
poetry. The main difference between these metres and the
ordinary *dróttkvætt* is that the number of syllables in each line
can vary (usually they are shorter than in *dróttkvætt*) and each
line ends on a stressed syllable (see p. 110). Rather than interpreting this as a variation of the *dróttkvætt* metre, Einar Ólafur
Sveinsson[36] argues that it is an innovation in itself, thus dismis-
sing the terminology of Snorri Sturluson who calls these metres
stýfðir, indicating that the lines have been shortened. Einar
Ólafur Sveinsson describes the nature of these metres and
discusses them in view of J. Carney's studies of accentual poetry
in Old Irish[37] as opposed to syllabic. Einar Ólafur Sveinsson
draws attention to three main points: First that each line ends in
a stressed syllable, secondly that there are four lifts in each line
and thirdly that lifts can fall on syllables which are unstressed in

---

34 Ibid, (1976) xxviii.
35 (1975) 171-217. For an abridged English version, see (1976).
36 (1975) 185).
37 Ibid, 201-04.

normal speech.[38] He thinks that the similarity is too extraordinary to be accidental and the difference in the usage of alliteration and *hendingar* can be explained by the fact that these had already developed in Scandinavian poetry.[39] Einar Ólafur Sveinsson suggests that the rhythm could have been borrowed by Norsemen who heard the Irish metres accompanied by music, thus making it easier for them to get an idea of the rhythm.[40] He then proceeds to look at the earliest named authors of poetry in *hnepptir hættir* showing that these could have had some connections in the west (Þórir snepill whose father is said to have been in the Scottish Isles and Kormákr who has been mentioned above — see p. 95-97).

As for Irish origins of *dróttkvætt* itself, Einar Ólafur says that this still needs to be proved.[41]

38 Ibid, (1975) 204; (1976) 148. At the Viking Conference in Dublin 1973, Einar Ólafur Sveinsson and James Carney put on a little performance: "At this point the speaker broke off the reading of his paper with the words: "Now I should very much like to call upon my friend and colleague Professor James Carney to help me to make an experiment. He has kindly consented to read an Old Irish accentual stanza, and I shall read a Northern catalectic semistrophe". Professor Carney now ascended the podium. Then the speaker read a semistrophe from the fragment ascribed to King Harold [...]:

Hneggi ber ek æ ugg;
Ótta hlýði mær drótt
(dána vek ek dular mey)
drauga á kerlaug.

And Professor Carney answered by reciting an Old Irish accentual stanza:

Canaid cuí céol mbind mbláith
dia mbí súan sáim réid;
lengait éoin ciúin crúaich
ocus daim lúath léith.

Then a change was made in the recitation. The speaker read line one of his semistrophe, and Professor Carney line one of his stanza, then came line two in both examples, and so they proceeded to the end of the verses. Then the lecturer continued to read his paper." (Einar Ólafur Sveinsson (1976) 148).

39 Ibid, (1975) 204-05.
40 Ibid, 205-06.
41 Ibid, 212.

8.3.3. MacKenzie's Studies

B.G. MacKenzie[42] has recently reviewed Turville-Petre's studies, claiming that some of the "sharp differences" emphasised by him "seem sharper because late forms of Irish verse have been compared with late forms of scaldic, when each had become more stylized and less flexible. Scaldic poetry of the ninth and tenth centuries must be seen alongside its Irish contemporaries."[43]

Looking at alliteration, MacKenzie shows that in earlier scaldic verse this was far from being as strict as it later became. She quotes various examples which all indicate that the rule of 2 *stuðlar* in the first line and 1 *hǫfuðstafr* in the second (2+1) is a later development. Instances of three-line binding are also quoted (1+2+1) and claimed to show similarities to early non-syllabic Irish verse.[44] In conclusion she says that some Irish elements were undeniably "present in scaldic alliteration, and they cannot be explained as part of the common Germanic tradition."[45]

Rhyme was also used much more freely in the early decades of scaldic poetry than later. MacKenzie mentions examples of rhyme within one line (horizontal rhyme) and between lines (vertical rhyme) in various early scaldic poems as well as elaborate but unsystematised rhyme in longer poems.[46] For this practice she finds Irish parallels, especially in the Irish *aicill* rhyme[47] where the final word of one line rhymes with a word in the next.[48] Instances of this device in scaldic poetry are numer-

42 (1981).
43 Ibid, 338.
44 Ibid, 340.
45 Ibid, 341.
46 Ibid, 341ff.
47 Einar Ólafur Sveinsson (1975) 211 mentioned this as a possible likeness which had to be further investigated.
48 B.G. Mac Kenzie (1981) 346ff.

ous from Bragi the Old onwards. Various forms of *aicill* rhyme in Old Icelandic are described along with "alliterative Binding."[49] These interact and can be combined according to individual taste not following any discernable rules. "The Irish poets of the same period combined the two devices in almost exactly the same way; perhaps they used slightly less Binding and a little more *aicill* than did the skalds, but the patterns are very similar."[50] MacKenzie even shows a tendency among the early scalds to let consonants of similar phonetic quality rhyme thus making them closer to the Irish (see p. 110).

With regard to stress, MacKenzie argues that there is no evidence of a fixed stress-pattern in scaldic poetry. Since every syllable of a line could carry alliteration and rhyme the same should apply to stress. With this in mind, scaldic poetry shows "patterns remarkably like those of Irish poetry."[51] She also discusses evidence of Old Irish poetry being accompanied by music and claims that the same could apply to scaldic verse. This could, she claims, explain "the apparently haphazard stressing of what appear to be unimportant words in skaldic verse [...and] also the varying role of *ek*, which seems to have full syllabic status even after a vowel in some lines."[52] Here, however, we have no evidence of any scaldic music so little can be said either to support or to refute the suggestion.

MacKenzie does not doubt the authenticity of the so-called earliest scaldic poetry and therefore arrives at the conclusion that the introduction of scaldic metres on the basis of Irish metres took place in the ninth century and was further reinforced by "Norse-Irish contacts in the large bi-lingual Gall-Gael population in Ireland and the Hebrides during the skaldic period."[53]

49 Ibid, 350.
50 Ibid, 351.
51 Ibid, 353.
52 Ibid, 355.
53 Ibid, 356.

8.3.4. Kristján Árnason's Studies

In the latest study on the subject, Kristján Árnason[54] has emphasised that the rhythm is much more central to scaldic metres than patterns of alliteration and rhyme as studied by MacKenzie. This he compares with what can be found in the Old Irish metre *rinnard* (four six-syllable lines with a trochaic ending) and refers to studies by C. Watkins[55] and J. Carney[56] which show that syllable counting in Old Irish poetry was a later development.[57] Kristján Árnason postulates a somewhat similar view for scaldic poetry, saying:

[...] there is reason to believe that the basic character of the rhythm was not simply a mechanic counting of syllables, but that stress and quantity played a central role, and that it is an incidental fact that the number of syllables in most dróttkvætt lines was six.[58]

Kirstján Árnason analyses several lines of twelfth century poetry where the basic form is a combination of three trochees. Heavy beats have to be carried by syllables which are both heavy and stressed in ordinary speech. In some instances at least, irregularity in the number of syllables in each line may be accounted for by the suggestion that one strong beat equals two light ones.

Talking about the general likelihood of metres being borrowed from one language to another, Kristján Árnason points out that both Old Irish and Old Norse had initial word stress with the exception of Old Irish compounds with the main stress on the first syllable of the second element in the word. Both languages distinguished between long and short stressed vowels

54 (1981).
55 (1963).
56 (1971).
57 Kristján Árnason (1981) 103.
58 Ibid, 103.

and these features, he says, could affect metrical rhythm and thus make it easier for Irish metres to find their way into Old Norse.[59] Apparently, quantity does not play the same role in the *rinnard* as in the *dróttkvætt*:

[...] it seems to have been the case with the rinnard metre (unlike dróttkvætt) that both heavy and light syllables could carry the ictus of the trochaic ending of the line:

> Cros Chríst tar mo láma (heavy)
> óm gúallaib com basa (light)
> Cros Chríst tar mo lesa (light)
> Cros Chríst tar mor chasa (light).[60]

Kristján Árnason also discusses how the metre was remodelled in the hypothetical borrowing process, pointing out, as earlier scholars have done, that both traditions have developed independently. In conclusion he says:

Although it can hardly be said that any proof has been given that Stokes was right in asserting that the Old-Norse court poets imitated the rinnard, it seems far from unlikely that something of this kind occurred.[61]

Even though we cannot prove that scaldic metres originated in Irish metres, it should be remembered that we cannot prove either that scaldic metres originated in Norway. But the simplest explanation of the peculiar nature of scaldic poetry and of the fact that most scaldic poets came from Iceland, is that the genre was influenced by the Gaels in Iceland and created in the poetic tradition brought to that country from Ireland and Scotland.

---

59 Ibid, 107-09.
60 Ibid, 108.
61 Ibid, 110. The reference to Stokes is from (1885).

Chapter IX

CONCLUSIONS

The literary heritage which was brought from Scandinavia to Iceland during the Age of Settlement was probably closely akin to what may be found in some of the Eddaic poems. These poems are concerned with the Scandinavian gods and ancient heroes of Germanic and Scandinavian origin. As there is no evidence of a strong oral prose narrative tradition in Scandinavia at such an early date it is unlikely that such a tradition in Iceland should be traced to Scandinavia. In Iceland, however, a reasonable proportion of the population was Gaelic, coming from a cultural area where oral prose narrative was already well established. Most of these Gaels were slaves and we have seen that more often than not they were given Scandinavian names by their Norse masters. Since not even their names were tolerated, we may assume that their language was not tolerated either, and this may account for the apparently few Gaelic loanwords in Icelandic. It is likely that the slaves were obliged to learn the language of their masters.

Due to the nature of the situation it can also be suggested that it must have been unacceptable to use Gaelic heroes in the stories which these slaves would have told. They could nevertheless have told stories which reflected their literary tastes and used motifs and ideas from their Gaelic material in a Scandinavian context. If this were indeed the case, the Gaelic stories as such must have been forgotten after one or two generations. This explains why no Gaelic heroes or stories appear in Old Icelandic literature. But the art of storytelling *per se* survived and developed.

It is therefore not surprising that most of the Gaelic ideas and motifs in Old Icelandic literature are found in the material which most closely resembles the oldest tradition in Iceland, namely the *Fornaldarsögur* and the mythological material. It would appear likely, then, that the *Fornaldarsögur*, to a great extent, were founded on older poetic lore which was then transposed into oral prose narrative in Iceland. The framework for the mythological tales on the other hand, as we know them from Snorri's Prose-Edda and the Eddaic poems, is no doubt Scandinavian. Within that frame, however, stories could be added and changed thus allowing for Gaelic motifs to penetrate the mythology and be attached to the Scandinavian gods.

The literary genres which developed in Iceland, such as the Kings' Sagas and the Family Sagas, show fewer traces of the Gaelic influence, though such traces may be found in some Family Sagas which come from areas where Gaels are known to have been prominent.

Scaldic poetry fits well into this general frame. This art was mainly practised by Icelanders and most named poets came from areas where Gaels are known to have been among the first settlers. There is also evidence to suggest that the art of scaldic poetry was acquired through special training, though this seems to have been confined to certain families and not to have taken place in professional schools as in Ireland. Moreover, scaldic metres differ considerably from older Germanic and Scandinavian metres but show marked similarities to those found in Old Irish poetry.

Nothing comes from nothing. All explanations founded on indigeneous development fail to account for the strength of Icelandic literary tradition in comparison to that in Norway. The theory of a subsidiary Gaelic influence seems the most satisfactory.

BIBLIOGRAPHY

LIST OF ABBREVIATIONS

AIT
  Ancient Irish Tales ed. by Cross, T.P., and Slover, C.H., Allen Figgis, Dublin, 1968 (first ed. in 1936).
DIAS
  The Dublin Institute for Advanced Studies.
Edda
  Norræn fornkvæði ed. by Sophus Bugge, Christiania, 1867.
FAS
  Fornaldarsögur Norðurlanda vol. I-IV, ed. by Guðni Jónsson, Reykjavík, 1959 (repr. of 1950 ed.).
ÍF
  Íslenzk fornrit (Hið íslenzka fornritafélag), Reykjavík.
MMIS
  Mediaeval and Modern Irish Series.
RIA
  Royal Irish Academy.
Skjd.
  Den Norsk-Islandske Skjaldedigtning AI, ed. by Finnur Jónsson, Copenhagen, 1912.

PRIMARY SOURCES

Aided Chonchobuir
1906
  The Death of Conchobar ed. and transl. by Meyer, K., in *The Death-Tales of the Ulster Heroes* (RIA, Todd Lecture Series, vol. XIV), Dublin, 2-21 (also in AIT, 343-46).
Aided Fergusa maic Roich
1906
  The Death of Fergus mac Roich ed. and transl. by Meyer, K., in *The Death-Tales of the Ulster Heroes* (RIA, Todd Lecture Series, vol. XIV), Dublin, 32-35.

121

Aided Óenfir Aífe
1956
The Death of Aífe's Only Son ed. by van Hamel, A.G. in Compert Con Culainn DIAS (MMIS 3), Dublin, 9-15 (transl. in Gantz, J., (1981) 147-52).
Aislinge Óenguso
1934
Ed. by Shaw, F., Browne and Nolan Ltd., London (transl. in Gantz, J., (1981), The Dream of Óengus, 107-12.
Ála flekks saga
1927
Ed. by Lagerholm Å., in Drei Lygisǫgur Halle, 84-120.
Anderson, A.O. (ed. and transl.)
1922
Early Sources of Scottish History A.D. 500-1286 vol I, Oliver and Boyd, Edinburgh/London.
Annals of Ireland. Three Fragments, copied from Ancient Sources
1860
Ed. and transl. by O'Donovan, J., Dublin.
Annals of the Kingdom of Ireland by the Four Masters
1851
Ed. and transl. by O'Donovan, J., Dublin.
Annals of Ulster
1887
Ed. and transl. by Hennessy, W.M., Dublin.
1983
Ed. and transl. by Seán Mac Airt and Gearóid Mac Niocaill, DIAS, Dublin.
Baldrs draumar
1867
Ed. in Edda, 135-38.
Bandamanna saga
1936
Ed. by Guðni Jónsson, in ÍF 7, 293-363.
Bárðar saga Snæfellsáss
1953
Ed. by Guðni Jónsson in Íslendingasögur III (Íslendingasagnaútgáfan), Reykjavík, 295-355.
Bellows, H.A, (transl.),
1968
The Poetic Edda (fifth printing), The American-Scandinavian Foundation, New York (first ed. 1923).
Bjarnar saga Hítdælakappa
1938
Ed. by Sigurður Nordal and Guðni Jónsson in ÍF 3, 111-211.

The Book of Leinster
1954-83
Vol. I, ed. by Best, R.I., Bergin, O., and O'Brien, M.A. (1954); Vol. II-V, ed. by Best, R.I., and O'Brien, M.A. (1956, 1957, 1965, 1967); Vol. VI, ed. by O'Sullivan, A. (1983), DIAS, Dublin.

Brennu-Njáls saga
1954
Ed. by Einar Ólafur Sveinsson in ÍF 12.

Bricriu's Feast
see
Fled Bricrend.

Caithréim Cellaig
1971
Ed. by Mulchrone, K., DIAS (MMIS 24), Dublin (also in *Silva Gadelica* 49-65 and 50-69 in translation).

The Canterbury Tales
1957
Ed. by Robinson, F.N., in *The Works of Geoffrey Chaucer* Oxford University Press (2nd ed.).

Cath Maige Turedh
1891
"The Second Battle of Moytura", ed. and transl. by Stokes, W., in *Revue Celtique* XII, 52-130.

Cattle Raid of Cualnge
see
Táin Bó Cúailnge.

Chronicum Scotorum
1866
Ed. by Hennessy, W.H. (Rolls Series 46), London.

Cogadh Gaedhel re Gallaibh
1867
The War of the Gaedhil with the Gaill ed. and transl. by Todd, J.H. (Rolls Series 48), London.

Colgrave, B., and Mynors, R.A.B. (eds.),
1969
Bede's Ecclesiastical History of the English People Oxford at the Clarendon Press.

Comracc Líadaine ocus Cuirithir
1902
Liadain and Curithir — An Irish Love-Story of the Ninth Century ed. by Meyer, K., London.

Cross T.P., and Slover C.H. (eds.),
1969

Ancient Irish Tales Allen Figgis, Dublin (first published in 1936).
Da Derga's Hostel
see
Togail Bruidne Da Derga.
Darraðarljóð
1912
Ed. in Skjd., 419-21.
Den Norsk-Islandske Skjaldedigtning AI
1912
Ed. by Finnur Jónsson, Copenhagen.
De Chophur in da Muccida
1979
Dialogue of The Two Swineherds ed. and transl. by Roider, U. (Innsbrucker Beiträge zur Sprachwissenschaft 28), Innsbruck.
Echtra Airt meic Cuind
1907
"The Adventures of Art son of Conn, and the Courtship of Delbchaem", ed. and transl. by Best, R.I., in *Ériu* III, 149-73 (also in AIT, 491-502).
Echtra Connla mac Cuinn
1927
"Conle's Abenteuerliche Fahrt", ed. and transl. by Pokorny, J., in *Zeitschrift für Celtische Philologie* XVII, 193-205 (also in AIT *The Adventures of Connla the Fair*, 488-90.
Echtra mac Echach
1903
"The Death of Crimthann son of Fidach, and the Adventures of the sons of Eochaid", ed. and transl. by Stokes, W., in *Revue Celtique* 24, 172-207. "Echtra mac Echach" on 190-207 (also in AIT, 508-13).
Echtra Nerai
1889/1890
"The Adventures of Nera", ed. and transl. by Meyer, K., in *Revue Celtique* X/XI, 212-28/209-10 (also in AIT, 248-53).
Egils saga ok Ásmundar
1959
Egils saga einhenda ok Ásmundar berserkjabana in FAS III, 323-65.
Egils saga
1933
Egils saga Skalla-Grímssonar ed. by Sigurður Nordal in ÍF 2.
Eiríks saga víðförla
1860
Ed. in *Flateyjarbók* I, Christiania, 29-36.
Eyrbyggja saga
1935

Ed. by Einar Ólafur Sveinsson and Matthías Þórðarson in ÍF 4.
The Fate of the Children of Tuireann
1863
Ed. by O'Curry, E., in *Atlantis* 4, 157-227.
Finn and the Man in the Tree
1904
Ed. and transl. by Meyer, K., in *Revue Celtique* 25, 344-49.
Fisher, P. (transl.),
1979
Saxo Grammaticus — The History of the Danes ed. by Davidsson, H.E., and Brewer, D.S., Cambridge.
Fjölsvinnsmál
1867
Ed. in Edda, 343-351.
Flateyjarbók I/II
1860/1862
Christiania
Fled Bricrend
1899
The Feast of Bricriu ed. and transl. by Henderson, G. (The Irish Text Society II), London.
do Fogluim Chonculainn
1908
"The Training of Cúchulainn", ed. and transl. by Stokes, W., in *Revue Celtique* 29, 109-52.
Fóstbrœðra saga
1943
Ed. by Björn K. Þórólfsson and Guðni Jónsson in ÍF 6, 121-276.
Gantz, J.,
1981
Early Irish Myths and Sagas Penguin Classics.
Grettis saga
1936
Grettis saga Ásmundarsonar ed. by Guðni Jónsosn in ÍF 7.
Griplur
1909-10
Ed. by Finnur Jónsson in *Rímnasafn* 4-5, Copenhagen, 351-410.
Grógaldr
1867
Ed. in Edda, 338-342.
Gwynn, E (ed. and transl.),
1903
The Metrical Dindsenchas Part I (RIA, Todd Lecture Series, vol. VIII) Dublin.

125

Hákonarmál
1912
Ed. in Skjd., 64-68.
Hálfdanar saga Brönufóstra
1959
Ed. in FAS IV, 287-318.
Hálfdanar saga svarta
1941
Ed. by Bjarni Aðalbjarnarson in *Heimskringla* I, ÍF 26, 84-93.
Hálfs saga ok Hálfsrekka
1959
Ed. in FAS II, 93-134.
Haraldskvæði (Hrafnsmál)
1912
Ed. in Skjd., 24-29.
Háttalykill
1912
Ed. in Skjd., 512-28.
Haustlǫng
1912
Ed. in Skjd., 16-20.
Heimskringla I
1941
Ed. by Bjarni Aðalbjarnarson in ÍF 26.
Helga þáttr Þórissonar
1959
Ed. in FAS IV, 345-53.
Helgakviða Hjörvarðssonar
1867
Ed. in Edda, 171-78.
Helgakviða Hundingsbana II
1867
Ed. in Edda, 190-201.
Historia Danica
1839
Saxonis Grammatici Historia Danica Copenhagen.
Hjálmþérs saga
1959
Hjálmþés saga ok Ölvis ed. in FAS IV, 177-243.
Hrólfs saga Gautrekssonar
1959
Ed. in FAS IV, 51-176.
Hrómundar saga
1959

126

Hrómundar saga Gripssonar ed. in FAS II, 405-22 (this saga is based on
Griplur).
Högna þáttr
1959
Sörla þáttr eða Héðins saga ok Högna ed. in FAS I, 367-82.
The Intoxication of the Ulstermen
see
Mesca Ulad.
Íslendingabók
see
Landnámabók.
Jackson, K.H. (ed. and transl.),
1951
A Celtic Miscellany Routledge & Kegan Paul.
Ketils saga hængs
1959
Ed. in FAS II, 149-181.
Kjalnesinga saga
1959
Ed. by Jóhannes Halldórsson in ÍF 14.
Konungs Skuggsjá
1848
Kongespeilet ed. by Keyser, R., Munch, P.A., and Unger, C.R., Christiania.
Kormáks saga
1939
Ed. by Einar Ólafur Sveinsson in ÍF 8, 203-302.
Krákumál
1912
Ed. in Skjd., 641-49.
Lagerholm, Å. (ed.),
1927
Drei Lygisǫgur Halle.
Landnámabók
1968
Ed. by Jakob Benediktsson in *Íslendingabók-Landnámabók* ÍF 1.
Laxdæla saga
1934
Ed. by Einar Ólafur Sveinsson in ÍF 5.
Lebor na hUidre: Book of the Dun Cow
1929
Ed. by Best, R.I., and Bergin, O., Dublin.
Ljósvetninga saga
1940

Ed. by Björn Sigfússon in ÍF 10.
The Mabinogion
1949
Transl. by Gwyn Jones and Thomas Jones (Everyman's Library 97).
McGrew, J.H. (transl.),
1974
Sturlunga saga II, transl. by McGrew, J.H,. and Thomas, G.,(The Library of Scandinavian Literature, vol. 10), The American Scandinavian Foundation, New York.
Magnusson, Magnus and Pálsson, Hermann (transl.),
1960
Njal's Saga Penguin Classics.
The Marriage of Sir Gawain
1882
Ed. by Child, F.J., in *The English and Scottish Popular Ballads* I, Boston and New York, Houghton, Mifflin and Company, 288-96.
Mesca Ulad
1941
The Intoxication of the Ulstermen ed. by Watson, J.C. DIAS (MMIS 13), Dublin (also in AIT, 215-38).
Mittelirische Verslehren
1891
Ed. by Thurneysen, R., in *Irische Texte* III 1, ed. by Stokes, W., and Windisch, E., Leipzig, 5-106.
Njáls saga
see
Brennu-Njáls saga.
Norræn fornkvæði
1867
Ed. by Sophus Bugge, Christiania.
Óláfs saga helga
1945
ór Óláfs sǫgu ins helga inni sérstǫku ed. by Bjarni Aðalbjarnarson in *Heimskringla* II, ÍF 27, 419-451.
Ólafs saga Tryggvasonar
1932
Saga Óláfs Tryggvasonar af Oddr Snorrason munk ed. by Finnur Jónsson, Copenhagen.
Olrik, J. (transl.),
1925
Sakses Danesaga I-II, Copenhagen.
Orkneyinga saga
1965

128

Ed. by Finnbogi Guðmundsson in ÍF 34.
Pálsson, Hermann, and Edwards, P. (transl.),
1972
The Book of Settlements (University of Manitoba Icelandic Studies, vol I),
Winnipeg.
Pálsson, Hermann (transl.),
1975
The Confederates and Hen-Thorir (The New Saga Library), Southside,
Edinburgh.
Pálsson, Hermann, and Edwards, P. (transl.),
1976
Egil's saga Penguin Classics.
Poetic-Edda
see
Norræn fornkvæði
Ragnarsdrápa
1912
Ed. in Skjd., 1-4.
Rennes Dindsenchas
1894
"The Prose Tales in the Rennes Dinsenchas", ed. and transl. by Stokes, W.,
in *Revue Celtique* 15, 272-336/418-84.
Rígsþula
1867
Ed. in Edda, 141-49.
Scéla Mucce Meic Dathó
1935
Ed. by Thurneysen, R. (DIAS, MMIS, vol. 6), Dublin (transl. in J. Gantz
(1981), 179-87, *The Tale of Macc Da Thó's Pig*).
Serglige Con Culainn
1953
Ed. by M. Dillon DIAS (MMIS 14), Dublin (transl. in AIT *The Sickbed of Cu
Chulainn*, 176-98).
Sigrdrífumál
1867
Ed. in Edda, 227-34.
Silva Gadelica — A Collection of Tales in Irish (2 vols.)
1892
Ed. and transl. by O'Grady, S.H., London.
Skáldskaparmál
see
Snorra-Edda.

129

Skarðsárbók
1958
Ed. by Jakob Benediktsson, Reykjavík.
Snorra-Edda
1931
Edda Snorra Sturlusonar ed. by Finnur Jónsson, Copenhagen.
Storm, G. (ed.),
1880
"Historia de Antiquitate Regum Norwagiensium" in *Monumenta Historica Norvegiæ* Kristiania (repr. 1973).
Sturlunga saga I
1946
Ed. by Jón Jóhannesson, Magnús Finnbogason and Kristján Eldjárn, Reykjavík.
Sveins rímur Múkssonar
1948
Ed. in *Rit Rímnafélagsins* I, Reykjavík.
Sörla saga sterka
1959
Ed. in FAS III, 367-410.
Sörla þáttr eða Héðins saga ok Högna
1959
Ed. in FAS I, 365-82.
Táin Bó Cúailnge - Recension I
1976
Ed. and transl. by O'Rahilly, C., DIAS, Dublin.
Táin Bó Cúalnge — from the Book of Leinster
1967
Ed. and transl. by O'Rahilly, C., DIAS, Dublin.
Táin Bó Fraích
1974
Ed. by Meid, W. DIAS (MMIS 22), Dublin (transl. in J. Gantz (1981). *The Cattle Raid of Fróech*, 114-26).
Tierney, J.J. (ed. and transl.),
1967
Dicuili Liber de Mensura Orbis Terrae DIAS (Scriptores Latini Hiberniae 6), Dublin.
Tochmarc Étaíne
1938
"The Wooing of Étaín", ed. and transl. by Bergin, O. and Best, R.I., in *Ériu* 12, 137-96 (also in AIT, 82-91).

Togail Bruidne Da Derga
1963
Ed. by Knott, E. DIAS (MMIS, vol. 8), Dublin (transl. in AIT, 93-126, *The Destruction of Da Dergas Hostel*).
Topographia Hibernica
1867
By Giraldus Cambrensis, ed. by Dimock, J.F. in *Giraldi Cambrensis Opera* vol. V (Rolls Series 21), (transl. by O'Meara, Penguin Classics, 1982).
Ungen Svejdal
1856
Ed. by Grundtvig, S. (with additional commentary by S. Bugge) in *Danmarks Gamle Folkeviser* vol II, no 70, Copenhagen.
Vatnsdœla saga
1939
Ed. by Einar Ólafur Sveinsson in ÍF 8.
The Voyage of Bran son of Febal
1895
Ed. and transl. by Meyer, K., London.
Völsunga saga
1959
Ed. in FAS I, 107-218.
Völuspá
1867
Ed. in Edda, 1-26.
Völuspá in skamma
1968
Ed. by Ólafur Briem in *Eddukvæði* (Íslenzk úrvalsrit 5), Skálholt, 510-13.
The War of the Gaedhil with the Gaill
see
Cogadh Gaedhel re Gallaibh.
Ynglinga saga
1941
Ed. by Bjarni Aðalbjarnarson in *Heimskringla* I, ÍF 26, 9-83.
Þórsdrápa
1912
Ed. in Skjd., 148-52.
Þorsteins saga Síðu-Hallssonar
1950
Ed. by Jón Jóhannesson in *Austfirðinga sögur*, ÍF 11, 299-320.
Þorsteins þáttr bœjarmagns
1959
Ed. in FAS IV, 319-344.

131

Örvar-Odds saga
1959
Ed. in FAS II, 199-363.

SECONDARY SOURCES

Aðalsteinsson, Stefán,
1981
"Origin and conservation of farm animal populations in Iceland", in *Z. Tierz Zucht Biol.* 98, 258-64.
1982
"Uppruni íslenskra húsdýra", in *Eldur er í norðri*, ed. by S. Steinþórsson, Reykjavík.
1985
"Possible changes in the frequency of the human ABO blood groups in Iceland due to smallpox epidemics selection", in *Annals of Human Genetics* 49, 275-81.
Agnarsdóttir, Anna, and Árnason, Ragnar,
1983
"Þrælahald á þjóðveldisöld", in *Saga* 21, 5-26.
Andersson, T.M.,
1964
The Problem of Icelandic Saga Origins New Haven and London, Yale University Press.
Almqvist, Bo,
1965
"The Viking Ale and the Rhine Gold. Some Notes on an Irish-Scottish Folk-Legend and a Germanic Hero-Tale Motif", in *Arv* 21, 115-35.
1966
"'Er konungsgarðr rúmur inngangs, en þrøngr brottfarar' — Ett forn-isländskt ordspråk och dess iriska motstycke", in *Arv 22, 173-93*.
1981
"Scandinavian and Celtic Folklore Contacts in the Earldom of Orkney", in *Saga-Book* XX (1978-81), 80-105.
Árnason, Kristján,
1981
"Did *dróttkvætt* Borrow its Rhythm from Irish?", in *Íslenskt mál* 3, 101-11.
Bekker-Nielsen, H., Olsen, T.D. and Widding, O.,
1965
Norrøn fortællekunst Akademisk forlag.

Bell, J.,
1985
"Last Sheaves, Ancient Cattle, and Protestant Bibles", in *Béaloideas* 53,
5-10.
Benediktsson, Jakob,
1968
"Formáli", in *Íslendingabók-Landnámabók* ed. by Jakob Benediktsson, ÍF 1.
1974
"Landnám og upphaf allsherjarríkis", in *Saga Íslands I*, Reykjavík, 153-96.
1983
Hugtök og heiti í bókmenntafræði Bókmenntafræðistofnun Háskóla Íslands,
Mál og menning, Reykjavík.
Bergin, O.,
1946
"White Red-Eared Cows", in *Ériu* 14, 170.
Berry, A.C.,
1974
"The Use of Non-Metrical Variations of the Cranium in the Study of Scan-
dinavian Population Movements", in *American Journal of Physical
Anthropology* 40, 345-58.
Berry, R.J.,
1977
"Comments on *The Settlement of Iceland*", in *Norwegian Archaeological
Review* 10, 66-68.
Bjarnason, O., Bjarnason, V., Edwards, J.H., Friðriksson, S., Magnússon, M.,
Mourant, A.E., Tills, D.,
1973
"The Blood Groups of Icelanders", in *Annals of Human Genetics* 36,
425-58.
Boberg I.M.,
1955
Baumeistersagen (Folklore Fellows Communications, 151), Helsinki.
Breatnach, P.A.,
1983
"The Chief's Poet", in *Proceedings of the RIA* 83 C, 37-79.
Brekkan, Ásmundur,
1954
"Blóðflokkar 3962 íslenzkra kvenna", in *Læknablaðið* 38, 138-44.
Brøgger, A.W.,
1929
Ancient Emigrants. A History of the Norse Settlements of Scotland Oxford at
the Clarendon Press.
1930

133

Den Norske Bosetning på Shetland-Orknøyene. Studier og Resultater Oslo.

Bugge, A.,

1900

"Nordisk Sprog og Nordisk Nationalitet i Irland", in *Aarbøger for Nordisk Oldkyndighed og Historie* 15, 279-332.

1905

Vesterlandenes Indflydelse paa Nordboernes og særlig Nordmændenes ydre kultur, levesæt og samfundsforhold i Vikingetiden (Videnskabs-Selskabets Skrifter II, Historisk-filosofisk Klasse, 1904, No. 1), Christiania.

1908

"Havelok og Olav Trygvesøn" in *Aarbøger for Nordisk Oldkyndighed og Historie* 23, 233-72 (English transl. in *Saga-Book* VI (1910), 257-95 ("Havelok and Olaf Tryggvason")).

1912

Norges Historie Fremstillet for det Norske Folk vol. I, part 1, Kristiania.

1912*

"Norse Loan Words in Irish", in *Miscellany Presented to Kuno Meyer* Halle, 291-306.

1916

"Irsk paavirkning paa den Islandske Saga", in *Festskrift til Gerhard Gran* Kristiania, 17-31.

Bugge, S.,

1889

"Iduns Æbler", in *Arkiv för Nordisk Filologi, 4, 1-45.*

1896

Helge-Digtene. Studier over de Nordiske Gude- og Heltesagns Oprindelse II, Copenhagen (transl. by Dr. Schofield, *Home of the Eddic Poems*, London, Nutt, 1899).

1908

Norsk Sagaskrivning og Sagafortælling in Irland Kristiania.

Carney, J.,

1955

Studies in Irish Literature and History DIAS, Dublin.

1971

"Three Old Irish Accentual Poems" in *Ériu* 22, 23-80.

Chadwick, H.M. & N.K.,

1932

The Growth of Literature I, Cambridge University Press.

Chadwick, N.K.,

1955

"Pictish and Celtic Marriage in Early Literary Tradition", in *Scottish Gaelic Studies* VIII, 56-115.

1957

134

"Literary Tradition in the Old Norse and Celtic World", in *Saga-Book* XIV (1953-57), 164-99.
1970
The Celts Penguin Books.
Chesnutt, M.,
1968
"An unsolved problem in Old Norse-Icelandic Literary History", in *Mediaeval Scandinavia* I, 122-37.
Christiansen, R.Th.,
1930
The Vikings and the Viking Wars in Irish and Gaelic Tradition (Skrifter utg. av Det Norske Videnskabs-Akademi i Oslo, II, Historisk-Filosofisk Klasse No. 1), Oslo.
Ciklamini, M.,
1968
"Journeys to the Giant Kingdom", in *Scandinavian Studies* 40, 95-110.
1971
"The Problem of Starkaðr", in *Scandinavian Studies 43, 169-88.*
Coffey, G. and Armstrong, E.C.R.,
1910
"Scandinavian objects found at Islandbridge and Kilmainham", in *Proceedings of the RIA* 28 C, 107-22.
Collingwood, W.G.,
1927
"Christian Vikings", in *Antiquity* 1, 172-80.
Craigie, W.A.,
1894
"Oldnordiske Ord i de gaeliske Sprog", in *Arkiv för Nordisk Filologi* 10, 149-66.
1897
"Gaelic Words and Names in the Icelandic Sagas", in *Zeitschrift für Celtische Philologie* I, 439-54.
1897*
"The Gaels in Iceland", in *Proceedings of the Society of Antiquaries of Scotland* 3. ser. VII, 247-64.
Dillon, M.,
1948
Early Irish Literature (fourth impression, 1969) The University of Chicago Press.
Donegani, J.A., Dungal, N., Ikin, E.W., and Mourant, A.E.,
1950
"The Blood Groups of the Icelanders", in *Annals of Eugenics* 15, 47-52.

135

Duncan, A.A.M.,
1975
Scotland: The Making of the Kingdom Edinburgh.
Einarsson, Bjarni,
1961
Skáldasögur Reykjavík.
Eldjárn, Kristján,
1956
Kuml og haugfé úr heiðnum sið á Íslandi Reykjavík.
1966
"Bjöllurnar frá Kornsá og Brú", in *Árbók hins íslenzka fornleifafélags* (pr. 1967), 67-70.
Ekwall, E.,
1924
Introduction to the Study of Place-Names Cambridge.
Ellis, H.R.,
1941
"Fostering by Giants in Old Norse Sagas", in *Medium Ævum* 10, 70-85.
Falk, H.,
1893/1894
"Om Svipdagsmál", in *Arkiv för Nordisk Filologi* 9, 31-62; and 10, 26-82.
Faraday, W.,
1899
"On the Question of Irish Influence on Early Icelandic Literature, Illustrated from the Irish MSS. in the Bodleian Library", in *Memoirs and Proceedings of the Manchester Literary and Philosophical Society* 44, part I (1899-1900), 1-22.
Feilberg, H.F.,
1910
Bjærgtagen (Danmarks Folkeminder 5), Copenhagen.
Fenton, A.,
1978
The Northern Isles: Orkney and Shetland Edinburgh.
Foote, P.,
1977
"Þrælahald á Íslandi", in *Saga* 15, 41-74.
Fossenias, M.,
1943
"Sägnerna om trollen Finn och Skalle som byggmästare", in *Folkkultur* 3, 5-144.
Friðriksson, Þorvaldur,
1982

136

Keltiska hustyper på Island Göteborgs universitet (unpublished).
1985
"Keltnesk höfðadýrkun á Íslandi", in *Lesbók Morgunblaðsins* Oct. 26. and
Nov. 2.
Goedheer, A.J.,
1938
Irish and Norse Traditions about the Battle of Clontarf Haarlem.
Graham-Campbell, J.,
1976
"The Viking-Age Silver Hoards of Ireland", in *Proceedings of the Seventh
Viking Congress* (Held in Dublin, 15-21 August, 1973) ed. by Almqvist, Bo,
and Greene, D., Dublin, 39-74.
Guðmundsson, Barði.
1959
Uppruni Íslendinga Bókaútgáfa Menningarsjóðs, Reykjavík.
Guðmundsson, Helgi,
1967
Um Kjalnesinga sögu (Studia Islandica 26), Reykjavík.
Guðnason, Bjarni,
1977
"Theodoricus og íslenskir sagnaritarar", in *Sjötíu ritgerðir helgaðar Jakobi
Benediktssyni* I (Stofnun Árna Magnússonar, Rit 12), Reykjavík, 107-20.
Haliday, C.,
1881
The Scandinavian Kingdom of Dublin Dublin (repr. 1969 from 2nd ed. 1884
by Irish University Press, Shannon, with an Introduction by Ó Ríordáin, B.).
van Hamel, A.G.,
1933
"Óðinn Hanging on the Tree", in *Acta Philologica Scandinavica* 7, 260-88.
Hannesson, Guðmundur,
1925
Körpermasze und Körperproportionen der Isländer (Supplement to *Árbók
Háskóla Íslands*), Reykjavík.
Hermann, P.,
1922
Die Heldensagen des Saxo Grammaticus, Leipzig.
Hermannsdóttir, Margrét,
1982
"Fornleifarannsóknir í Herjólfsdal — Vestmannaeyjum 1971-81", in *Eyja-
skinna* I (Sögufélag Vestmannaeyja), 83-127.
Heusler, A.,
1913 (1969)

137

Die Anfänge der isländischen Saga (Abhandlungen der Preussischen Akademie der Wissenschaften, phil.-hist. Klasse, No. 9) (repr. in *Kleine Schriften* II, Berlin, 1969, 388-459).

Holtsmark, A.,

1939

"Vefr Darraðar", in *Maal og Minne*, 74-96.

1957

"Darraðarlióð", in *Kulturhistoriskt Lexikon för nordisk Medeltid II*, Malmö, col. 667-68.

1964

"Kongespeillitteratur", in *Kulturhistoriskt Lexikon för nordisk Medeltid IX*, Malmö, col. 61-68.

Hughes, K.,

1969

"Introduction", in *A History of Mediaeval Ireland* by Otway-Ruthven, A.J., London.

1972

Early Christian Ireland. Introduction to the Sources London.

Hull, E.,

1903

"The Irish Episodes in Icelandic Literature", in *Saga-Book* 3 (1901-03), 235-70.

Jackson, K.H.,

1964

The Oldest Irish Tradition: A Window on the Iron Age Cambridge University Press.

Jakobsen, J.,

1901

"Shetlandsøernes Stednavne", in *Aarbøger for nordisk Oldkyndighed og Historie* 16, 55-258.

Jóhannesson, Jón,

1956

Íslendinga saga I, Reykjavík.

Jónsson, Finnur,

1921

Norsk-islandske kultur-og sprogforhold i 9. og 10. árh. (Det kgl. danske Videnskabernes Selskab, historisk-filologiske Meddelelser III:2), Copenhagen.

1922

"Mera om Folkminnen och Filologi", in *Folkminnen och folktankar* 8, 129-32.

1923

138

Den oldnorske og oldislandske Litteraturs Historie II (2nd ed.), Copenhagen.
Jónsson, Guðni,
1959
"Formáli", in *Fornaldarsögur Norðurlanda* I, Íslendingasagnaútgáfan, Reykjavík (repr. of 1954 ed.).
Karlsson, Gunnar,
1975
"Frá þjóðveldi til konungsríkis", in *Saga Íslands* II, Reykjavík.
Kress, Helga,
1980
"Mjǫk mun þér samstaft þykkja — Um sagnahefð og kvenlega reynslu í Laxdæla sögu", in *Konur skrifa* Sögufélag, Reykjavík 97-109.
Lagerholm, Å.,
1927
Drei Lygisǫgur Halle.
Laxness, Halldór,
1965
"Mannlíf hér fyrir landnámstíð", in *Tímarit Máls og menningar* 26, 126-31 (repr. in *Vínlandspúnktar* Reykjavík, 1969, 125-42).
Liestøl, K.,
1929
Upphavet til den islendske ættesaga Instituttet for sammenlignende kulturforskning, Oslo.
Liungman, W.,
1942
"Finnsagenproblemet", in *Folkminnen och Folktankar* 29, 86-113 and 138-54.
Lucas, A.T.,
1966
"Irish-Norse Relations: Time for a Reappraisal?", in *Journal of the Cork Historical and Archaeological Society* 71, 62-75.
1967
"The Plundering and Burning of Churches in Ireland, 7th to 16th Century", in *North Munster Studies* ed. by Rynne, E., Limerick, 172-229.
Lukman, Niels,
1977
"An Irish Source and Some Icelandic *fornaldarsögur*", in *Mediaeval Scandinavia* 10, 41-57.
Mac Cana, P.,
1962
"The Influence of the Vikings on Celtic Literature", in *Proceedings of the International Conference of Celtic Studies* (Held in Dublin, 6-10. July, 1959), ed. by Ó Cúív, B., DIAS, Dublin, 78-118.
1974

"The Rise of the Later Schools of *Filidheacht*", in *Ériu* 25, 126-46.
MacKenzie, B.G.,
1981
"On the Relation of Norse Scaldic Verse to Irish Syllabic Poetry", in *Speculum Norroenum* ed. by Dronke, U., Helgadóttir, Guðrún P., Weber, G.W., Bekker-Nielsen, H., Odense University Press, 337-56.
Mallory, J.P.,
1982
"The Sword of the Ulster Cycle", in *Studies on Early Ireland: Essays in Honour of M.V. Duignan* ed. by Scott, B.G., Belfast, 99-114.
Magnusson, Magnus, and Pálsson, Hermann,
1969
"Introduction", in *Laxdæla saga* transl. by Magnus Magnusson and Hermann Pálsson, Penguin Classics.
Marstrander, C.J.S.,
1915
Bidrag til det norske Sprogs Historie i Irland (Videnskabsselskabets Skrifter, II, hist.-filos. Klasse, no. 5), Kristiania.
Matras, C.,
1958
"Atlantssiðir — Atlantsorð", in *Fróðskaparrit* 7, 73-101.
Meyer, K.,
1894
"The Irish Mirabilia in the Norse 'Speculum Regale'", in *Folk-lore* V, 299-316.
1918
"Nordisch-Irisches", in *Sitzungsberichte der Preussischen Akademie der Wissenschaften* 45, 1030-47.
Milroy, J.,
1977
"Starkaðr: An Essay in Interpretation", in *Saga-Book* 19, 118-38.
Murphy, G.,
1952
"On the Dates of two Sources used in Thurneysen's Heldensage", in *Ériu* 16, 145-56.
Murray, H.,
1983
Viking and Early Medieval Buildings in Dublin (British Archaeological Reports, British Series 119), Oxford.
Nordal, Sigurður,
1953(1968)
Sagalitteraturen (Nordisk Kultur VIII B), Copenhagen (Icel. Transl: *Um íslenzkar fornsögur* Reykjavík, 1968).

140

Nutt, A.,
1895-97
"The Happy Otherworld in the Mythico — Romantic Literature of the Irish.
The Celtic Doctrine of Re-birth. An Essay in Two Sections", in *The Voyage
of Bran son of Febal* I-II, ed. by Meyer, K., London.
Ó Corráin, D.,
1972
Ireland before the Normans Dublin.
1974
"*Caithréim Chellacháin Chaisil* History or Propaganda?" in *Ériu* 25, 1-69.
O'Curry, E.,
1862
"The "*Tri Thruaighe na Scéalaigheachta*", (i.e. the "*Three Most Sorrowful
Tales*") of Erinn. I. "*The Exile of the Children of Uisnech*"", in *Atlantis* 3,
377-422.
Olrik, A.,
1894
Sakses Oldhistorie — Norröne Sagaer og Danske Sagn Copenhagen.
1909
"At sidde på höj", in *Danske Studier*, 1-10.
1910
Danmarks Heltedikming II, Copenhagen.
1925
Nordisches Geistesleben Heidelberg (2nd ed. — Transl. of *Nordisk Aandsliv*
Copenhagen & Kristiania, 1907).
Olsen, M.,
1935
"Krákumál", in *Maal og Minne*, 78-80 (repr. in *Norrøne Studier* Oslo, 1938,
245-48).
Pálsson, Árni,
1932
"Um lok þrældóms á Íslandi", in *Skírnir* 106, 191-203.
Pálsson, Hermann,
1952
"Keltnesk mannanöfn í íslenzkum örnefnum", in *Skírnir* 126, 195-203.
1953
"Um Íra-örnefni", in *Skírnir* 127, 105-111.
1958
"Vesturvíking Hjörleifs", in *Saga* II (1954-58), 309-315.
1962
Sagnaskemmtun Íslendinga Reykjavík.
1964

141

"Um írsk atriði í Laxdæla sögu", in *Tímarit Máls og menningar* 25, 392-402.
1965
"Minnisgreinar um Papa", in *Saga* 112-22.
Panzer, F.,
1901
Hilde-Gudrun: eine sagen- und literaturgeschichtliche Untersuchung Halle.
Power, R.,
1985
"Journeys to the Otherworld in the Icelandic *Fornaldarsögur*", in *Folklore* 96, 156-75.
1985*
"'An Óige, an Saol agus an Bás', — *Feis Tighe Chonáin* and Þórr's Visit to Útgarða-Loki", in *Béaloideas* 53, 217-94.
Rafnsson, Sveinbjörn,
1974
Studier í Landnámabók (Bibliotheca Historica Lundensis 31), Lund.
Reinhard, J.R.,
1933
The Survival of Geis in Mediaeval Romance Halle, Max Niemeyer.
Rooth, A.B.,
1961
Loki in Scandinavian Mythology (Skrifter utg. af Kungl. Humanistiska Vetenskapssamfundet i Lund 61), Lund.
Ross, A.,
1959
"The Human head in Insular Pagan Celtic Religion", in *Proceedings of the Society of Antiquaries of Scotland* 91, 10-43.
1962
"Severed Heads in Wells: an Aspect of the Well Cult", in *Scottish Studies* VI i, 31-48.
1967
Pagan Celtic Britain. Studies in Iconography and Tradition London: Routledge and Kegan Paul; New York: Columbia University Press.
Ryan, J. (SJ),
1938
"The Battle of Clontarf", in *Journal of the Royal Society of Antiquaries in Ireland* 68, 1-50.
Rynne, E.,
1966
"The Impact of the Vikings on Irish Weapons", in *Atti de VI Congresso Internazionale delle Scienze Preistoriche e Protostoriche* Sezioni V-VIII, 181-85.

142

Saugstad, L.F.,
1977
"The Settlement of Iceland", in *Norwegian Archaeological Review* 10 no.
1-2, 60-65.
Sawyer, P.H.,
1962
The Age of the Vikings London (2nd ed. 1971).
1970
"The Vikings and the Irish Sea", in *The Irish Sea Province in Archaeology
and History* ed. by Moore, D., Cardiff, 86-92.
1982
Kings and Vikings: Scandinavia and Europe A.D. 700-1100 Methuen, London and New York.
Sayers, W.,
1985
"Konungs Skuggsjá: Irish marvels and the King's Justice", in *Scandinavian
Studies* 57 no. 2, 147-61.
Schlauch, M.,
1934
Romance in Iceland London.
Shetelig, H.,
1940
Viking Antiquities in Great Britain and Ireland I, Oslo.
Sigfússon, Björn,
1958
"Ísland í erlendum miðaldaheimildum fyrir 1200 og hafsvæði þess", in *Saga* 2
(1954-58), 452-98.
Sigurðsson, Gísli,
1985
"Latin Learning and Saga Writing", — an M.Phil. Seminar paper, delivered
on April 18th, 1985, and submitted to the Board of Medieval Studies,
U.C.D. as part of the requirements for the degree of Master of Philosophy in
Medieval Studies (unpublished).
Simpson, J.,
1963
"Grímr the Good — a Magical Drinking Horn", in *Études Celtiques* 10
(1962-63), 489-515.
1965
"Mímir: Two Myths or One?", in *Saga-Book* 16, 41-53.
1966
"Otherworld Adventures in an Icelandic Saga", in *Folklore* 77, 1-20.
Small, A.,
1976

143

"Norse Settlement in Skye", in *Les Vikings et leur Civilisation. Problemes Actuels* ed. by Boyer, R., (Bibliotheque Arctique et Antartique 5), Paris, Mouton, La Haye, 29-37.

Smith, A.H.,
1928
Place Names of the North Riding of Yorkshire Cambridge.

Smyth, A.P.,
1977
Scandinavian Kings in the British Isles 850-880 Oxford.

Sommerfelt, A.,
1957
De Norsk-irske Bystaters Undergang 1169-1171 (Avhandl. utg. av det Norske Videnskaps-Akademi i Oslo, II, Hist.-Filos. Klasse, no. 4), Oslo.
1958
"On the Norse Form of the Name of the Picts and the Date of the First Norse Raids on Scotland", in *Lochlann* I, 218-22.
1962
"The Norse Influence on Irish and Scottish Gaelic", in *Proceedings of the International Congress of Celtic Studies* (Held in Dublin, 6-10. July, 1959) ed. by Ó Cuív, B., DIAS, Dublin, 73-77.

Steenstrup, J.C.H.R.,
1878
Normannerne II, Copenhagen (repr. by Selskabet for Udgivelse af Kilder til dansk Historie, Copenhagen, 1972).

Steffensen, Jón,
1946(1975)
"Uppruni Íslendinga", in *Samtíð og saga* III b, Reykjavík (repr. in *Menning og meinsemdir* Reykjavík, (1975) 15-33.
1951(1975)
"Víkingar", in *Samtíð og saga* V b, Reykjavík (repr. in *Menning og meinsemdir* Reykjavík, (1975) 34-52.
1951*(1975)
"Nokkur atriði úr fornsögu Noregs", in *Samtíð og saga* V b, Reykjavík, (repr. in *Menning og meinsemdir* Reykjavík, (1975) 53-61.
1969(1975)
"Þættir úr líffræði Íslendinga"; in *Læknaneminn* (repr. in *Menning og meinsemdir* Reykjavík, (1975) 258-74.
1971(1975)
"Tölfræðilegt mat á líffræðilegu gildi frásagna Landnámu af ætt og þjóðerni landnemanna", in *Saga* 9, 21-39 (repr. in *Menning og meinsemdir* Reykjavík, (1975) 92-106.

Stokes W.,
1885

144

"On the Metre *rinnard* and the Calendar of Oengus as Illustrating the Irish Verbal Accent", in *Revue Celtique* 6, 273-97.

Sveinbjarnardóttir, Guðrún.
1972
"Papar", in *Mímir* 19, 5-23.

Sveinsson, Einar Ólafur,
1932
"Keltnesk áhrif á íslenzkar ýkjusögur", in *Skírnir* 106, 100-23.
1934
"Formáli", in *Laxdæla saga* ÍF 5.
1940
Um íslenzkar þjóðsögur Reykjavík.
1945
"Papar", in *Skírnir* 119, 170-203.
1954
"Formáli", in *Brennu-Njáls saga* ÍF 12.
1959
"Celtic Elements in Icelandic Tradition", in *Béaloideas* 25 (1957 — printed in Dublin 1959), 3-24.
1959* "Fornaldarsögur Norðurlanda", in *Kulturhistoriskt Lexikon för nordisk Medeltid* IV, Malmö, col. 499-507.
1962
Íslenzkar bókmenntir í fornöld Almenna bókafélagið, Reykjavík.
1965
Ritunartími Íslendingasagna Reykjavík.
1966
"Kormakr the Poet and His Verses", in *Saga-Book* 17, 18-60.
1975
Löng er för (Studia Islandica 34), Reykjavík.
1976
"An Old Irish Verse Form Wandering in the North", in *Proceedings of the 7th Viking Congress* (Held in Dublin, 15-21 August, 1973), ed. by Almqvist, Bo and Greene, D., Dublin, 141-52.

von Sydow, C.W.,
1907/1908
"Studier i Finnsägnen og besläktade byggmästarsägner", i *Fataburen*, (1907); 65-78/199-218; (1908): 19-27.
1910
"Tors färd til Utgård", in *Danske Studier*, 65-105/145-82.
1920
"Iriskt Inflytande på nordisk Guda- och Hjältesaga", in *Årsbok* (Vetenskaps-Societeten i Lund), 19-29.
1922

145

"Folkminneforskning och Filologi", in *Folkminnen och folktankar* 8, 75-123 (cont.: "Mera om Folkminnen och Filologi"), 132-48.

Thompson E.A.,
1973
"The Icelandic Admixture Problem", in *Annals of Human Genetics* 37, 69-80.
1978
"Comments on *The Settlement of Iceland*", in *Norwegian Archaeological Review* 11, 57-58.

Thurneysen, R.,
1891
"Erläuterungen", with *Mittelirische Verslehren* in *Irische Texte* III 1, ed. by Stokes, W., and Windisch, E,. Leipzig, 107-68.
1921
Die irische Helden- und Königssage Halle (Saale).
1936
"Baile in scál", in *Zeitschrift für celtische Philologie* 20, 213-27.

Turville-Petre, G.,
1953
Origins of Icelandic Literature Oxford.
1954
"Um dróttkvæði og írskan kveðskap", in *Skírnir* 128, 31-55.
1964
Myth and Religion of the North London.
1972
"*Dróttkvætt* and 'Irish Syllabic Measures", in *Nine Norse Studies* by G. Turville-Petre (transl. of (1954)), Viking Society, London, 154-78.
1976
Scaldic Poetry Oxford at the Clarendon Press.

Vogt, L.J.,
1896
Dublin som norsk By Christiania.

de Vries, J.,
1963
Heroic Song and Heroic Legend transl. by Timmer, B.J., London, Oxford University Press (orig. ed. in Holland 1959).

Wainwright, F.T.,
1962
"The Scandinavian Settlement", in *The Northern Isles* ed. by Wainwright, F.T., Nelson, 117-62.

Wallace, P.,
1982
"The Origins of Dublin", in *Studies on Early Ireland: Essays in honour of*

M.V. Duignan ed. by Scott, B.G., Belfast, 129-43.

1982*

"Carpentry in Ireland AD 900-1300 — The Wood Quay Evidence", in *Woodworking Techniques before A.D. 1500* ed. by McGrail, S. (British Archaeological Reports, International Series 129), Oxford, 263-99.

1985

"The Archaeology of Viking Dublin", in *The Comparative History of Urban Origins in Non-Roman Europe* ed. by Clarke, H.B., and Simms, A. (British Archaeological Reports, International Series 255), Oxford, 103-145.

Walsh, A.,

1922

Scandinavian Relations with Ireland during the Viking Period Dublin.

Watkins, C.,

1963

"Indo-European Metrics and Archaic Irish Verse", in *Celtica* 6, 194-249.

Westropp, T.J.,

1913

"Brasil and the Legendary Islands of the North Atlantic: Their History and Fable. A Contribution to the 'Atlantis' Problem", in *Proceedings of the Royal Irish Academy* 30 C (1912-13), 223-63.

Wijsman E.M.

1984

"Techniques for estimating genetic admixture and applications to the problem of the origin of the Icelanders and the Ashkenazi Jews", in *Human Genetics* 67, 441-48.

Williams, C.,

1937

Thraldom in Ancient Iceland, Chicago.

Wormald, C.P.,

1982

"Viking Studies: Whence and Whither?", in *The Vikings* ed. by Farrell, R.T., Phillimore & Co. Ltd., London and Chichester, 128-53.

Young, J.I.

1933

"Does Rígsþula betray Irish Influence?", in *Arkiv för nordisk Filologi* 49, 97-107.

1937

"Some Icelandic Traditions Showing Traces of Irish Influence", in *Études Celtiques* 2, 118-26.

1938

"Two of the Irish 'Mirabilia' in the King's Mirror", in *Études Celtiques* 3, 21-26.

147

1950
"A Note on the Norse Occupation of Ireland", in *History* 35, 11-33.
Zimmer, H.,
1891
"Über die frühesten Berührungen der Iren mit den Nordgermanen", in *Sitzungsberichte der Königlich Preussischen Akademie der Wissenschaften* 279-317.
Þorsteinsson, Björn,
1966
Ný Íslandssaga Reykjavík.

FURTHER READING

Aðalsteinsson, Jón Hnefill,
1986
"Írsk kristni og norræn trú á Íslandi á tíundu öld", in *Saga* 24, 205-221.
Aðalsteinsson, Stefán,
1987
"Líffræðilegur uppruni Íslendinga", in *Íslensk þjóðmenning* I ed. by Frosti F. Jóhannsson, Reykjavík, 15-29.
Almqvist, Bo,
1969
"Livsfisken och livslaxen — Några marginalbidrag till isländsk-iriska föreställningar om Hv og själ", in *Einarsbók — Afmæliskveðja til Einars Ól. Sveinssonar* Reykjavík, 17-27.
1970
"Midfjordingamärren — En folklig satir från sturlungatiden och dess bakgrund", in *Årsbok 1969-1970* (Kungl. Humanistiska Vetenskaps-Samfundet i Uppsala, 5-20.
1970*
"The Uglier Foot", in *Béaloideas* 37/38 (1969-70), 1-50.
1976
"The Death Forebodings of Saint Óláfr, King of Norway, and Rögnvaldur Brúsason, Earl of Orkney", in *Béaloideas* 42-44 (1974-76), 1-40.
1978
"Norska utburdsägner i västerled", in *Norveg* 21, 109-19.
Bandle, O.,
1977
"Die Ortsnamen der Landnámabók", in *Sjötíu ritgerðir helgaðar Jakobi Benediktssyni* I (Stofnun Árna Magnússonar, Rit 12), Reykjavík, 47-68.

Basil, R.S. and Megaw, E.M.,
1950
"The Norse Heritage on the Isle of Man", in *The Early Cultures of North-West Europe* (H.M. Chadwick, Memorial Studies), ed. by Fox, C. and Dickens, B., Cambridge University Press, 141-70.

Bucholz, P.,
1976
"Fornaldarsaga und mündliches Erzählen zur Wikingerzeit", in *Les Vikings et leur Civilisation*. *Problemes Actuels* ed. by Boyer, R. (Bibliotheque Arctique et Antarctique 5), Paris, Mouton, La Haye, 133-78.
1980
Vorzeitkunde. Mündliches Erzählen and Überliefern im mittelalterlichen Skandinavien nach dem Zeugnis von Fornaldarsaga und eddischer Dichtung (Skandinavische Studien 13), Karl Wachholtz Verlag, Neumünster.

Bugge, A.,
1900
Contributions to the History of the Norsemen in Ireland I-III (I "The Royal Race of Dublin"; II "Norse Elements in Gaelic Tradition of Modern Times"; III "Norse Settlements Round the Bristol Channel"), Videnskabsselskabets Skrifter. II. Historisk-filosofisk Klasse. No. 6, Christiania.
1909
"Entstehung und Glaubwürdigkeit der isländischen Saga", in *Zeitschrift für deutsche Altertum* 51, N.F. 39, 23-38.

Bugge, S.,
1894
Bidrag til den ældste Skaldedigtnings Historie Christiania.

Chadwick, N.K.,
1950
"Þorgerðr Hölgabrúðr and the trollaþing: a Note on the Sources", in *The Early Cultures of North-West Europe* (H.M. Chadwick, Memorial Studies), ed. by Fox, C., and Dickens, B., Cambridge University Press 397-417.
1962
"The Vikings and the Western World", in *Proceedings of the International Congress of Celtic Studies* (Held in Dublin, 6.-10. July, 1959), ed. by Ó Cuív, B., Dublin, 13-42.
1968
"Dreams in Early European Literature", in *Celtic Studies — Essays in Memory of Angus Matheson* ed. by Carney, J., and Greene, D., Barnes & Noble, Inc., New York, 33-50.

Charles B.G.,
1934
Old Norse Relations with Wales Cardiff, University of Wales Press.

149

Chesnutt, M.,
1970
"Norse-Celtic Bibliographical Survey: First Report", in *Mediaeval Sçandinavia* 3, 109-37.
Chesnutt, M., Erlingsson, Davíð,
1971
"Norse-Celtic Bibliographical Survey: Second Report", in *Mediaeval Scandinavia* 4, 119-59.
Christiansen, R.T.,
1924
"Bidrag til Spørsmaalet om Berøringen mellem keltisk og nordisk Tradition", in *Maal og Minne*, 49-64.
1928
"A Gaelic Fairytale in Norway", in *Béaloideas* I (1927-28), 107-14.
1930
"A Norwegian Fairytale in Ireland?", in Béaloideas II, 235-245.
1938
"Gaelic and Norse Folklore", in *Folk-liv*, 321-35.
1952
"Til Spørsmålet om forholdet mellem irsk og nordisk tradisjon", in *Arv* 8, 1-41.
1959
Studies in Irish and Scandinavian Folktales published for Coimisiún Béaloideasa Éireann (Irish Folklore Commision) by Rosenkilde and Bagger, Copenhagen.
1962
"The People of the North", in *Lochlann* II, 137-64.
Craigie, W.A.,
1903
"Notes on the Norse-Irish Question", in *Arkiv för nordisk Filologi* 19, 173-80.
Crawford, B.E.,
1987
Scandinavian Scotland (Scotland in the Early Middle Ages 2) Leceister University Press.
Dahlstedt, Karl-Hampus,
1962
"Gudruns sorg: Stilstudier över ett Edda motiv", in *Scripta Islandica* 13, 25-47.
Donahue, C.,
1941
"The Valkyries and the Irish War-Goddesses", in *Publications of the Modern*

Language Association of America 56, 1-12.

Erlingsson, Davíð, Chesnutt, M.,
1971
"Norse-Celtic Bibliographical Survey: Second Report", in *Mediaeval Scandinavia* 4, 119-59.

Erlingsson, Davíð,
1980
"Hjörleifur kvensami og Fergus mac Léité", in *Gripla* 4, 198-205.

Guðmundsson, Helgi,
1959
"Máki, mákur", in *Íslenzk tunga* 1, 47-53.
1960
"Sklokr", in *Íslenzk tunga* 2, 51-56.

Hallseth, B.T.,
1967
"Irland-Afsnittet i Konungs Skuggsiá", in *Maal og Minne*, 50-63.

Heiermeier, A.,
1941
"Zwei irisch-isländische Parallelen", in *Zeitschrift für celtische Philologie* 22, 58-66.

Henry, P.L.,
1958
"An Irish-Icelandic Parallel *Ferdomun/Karlsefni*", in *Ériu* 18, 158-59.
1959
"Líadan and Guðrún — An Irish-Icelandic Correspondence", in *Zeitschrift für celtische Philologie* 27 (1958-59), 221-22.
1960
"The Icelandic Prepositional System", in *Zeitschrift für vergleichende Sprachforschung* (Kuhns Zeitschrift) 76 (1960), 89-135.

Henry, F.,
1967
Irish Art during the Viking Invasions 800-1020 London.

Hollander, L.M.,
1952
"Two Unrecognized Celtic Names: Vagn Akason and Thorvald Tintein", in *Studies in Honor of Albert Morey Sturtevant* University of Kansas Press, 71-75.

Holtsmark, A.,
1962
"Fód Báis — Banaþúfa — Heillaþúfa", in *Lochlann* II, 122-27.

Jónsson, Finnur,
1895
"De ældste skjalde og deres kvad", in *Aarbøger for nordisk Oldkyndighed og*

Historie 10, 271-359.
1906
"Nordens fremmedforbindelser i vikingetiden", in *Nordisk Tidsskrift for Filologi* 14 (1905-06), 145-56.
Krappe, A.H.,
1928
"The Valkyrie Episode in the Njals Saga", in *Modern Language Notes* 43, 471-74.
1929
"Deux Épisodes de Provenance Celtique", in *Revue Celtique* 46, 130-33.
1930
"L'Origine Irlandaise d'un Épisode de la *Hálfs saga*", in *Revue Celtique* 47, 401-05.
Laxness, Halldór,
1973
"Forneskjutaut", in *Skírnir* 147, 5-30 (repr. in *Þjóðhátíðarrolla* Reykjavík, 1974, 15-74.
Lockwood, W.B.,
1961
"Word Taboo in Faroese. Remarks on Gaelic-Scandinavian Contacts and a Note on English *Ingle*", in *Transactions of the Philological Society*, 1-16.
1962
"Scottish Gaelic *ucas, ucsa (ugsa)*, a Scandinavian Loan", in *Scottish Gaelic Studies* 9, 128-31.
1977
"Some Traces of Gaelic in Faroese", in *Fróðskaparrit* 25, 9-25.
1978
"Chr. Matras' Studies on the Gaelic Element in Faroese: Conclusions and Results", in *Scottish Gaelic Studies* 13, 112-26.
Mac Eoin, G.S.,
1963
"Some Icelandic Loricae", in *Studia Hibernica* 3, 143-54.
McTurk, R.,
1976
"Ragnarr loðbrók in the Irish Annals?", in *Proceedings of the Seventh Viking Congress* (Held in Dublin 1973), ed. by Almqvist, Bo, and Greene, D., RIA, Dublin, 93-123.
1979
"An Irish Analogue to the Kráka-Episode of Ragnars Saga loðbrókar", in *Éigse* 17 (1977-79), 277-296.
Marstrander, C.J.S.,
1921
"Altirische Personennamen mit *Gilla*", in *Zeitschrift für celtische Philologie*

152

13, 1-2.
1924
"Skjæks Øl", in *Festskrift til Amund B. Larsen* Kristiania, 186-89.
1928
Randbemerkninger til det norsk-irske Spørsmål (Avhandlinger utgitt av det
Norske Videnskaps-Akademi i Oslo II. Hist.-Filos. Klasse. 1927. No. 4),
Oslo.
Marwick, E.W.,
1972
"Creatures of Orkney Legend and their Norse Ancestory", in *Norveg* 15,
177-204.
Matras, C.,
1934
"Papýli í Føroyum", in *Varðin* 14, 185-87.
1954
"Lámh chearr í føroyskum máli", in *Fróðskaparrit* 3, 60-77.
1955
"Soppur í føroyskum og sopp í írskum", in *Fróðskaparrit* 4, 15-31.
1956
"Gammalfærøsk ærgi, n., og dermed beslægtede ord", in *Namn och Bygd* 44,
51-67.
1956*
"Caigeann og køkja", in *Fróðskaparrit* 5, 98-107.
1957
"Drunnur", in *Fróðskaparrit* 6, 20-33.
1962
"Blak", in *Fróðskaparrit* 11, 7-14.
1981
"Korkadalur", in *Fróðskaparrit* 28/29, 78-80.
Meyer, K.,
1910
"The Irish Mirabilia in the Norse "Speculum Regale"", in *Ériu* 4, 1-16.
Morris, C.D.,
1979
"The Vikings and Irish Monasteries", in *Durham University Journal* 71,
175-85.
Mossé, F.,
1933
"Sur le Nom d'Homme *Ketill* en Scandinave", in *Revue Celtique* 50, 248-53.
Ó Corráin, D.,
1979
"High-kings, Vikings and other kings", in *Irish Historical Studies* 21
(1978-79), 283-323.

153

Oftedal, M.,
1962
"On the Frequency of Norse Loanwords in Scottish Gaelic", in *Scottish Gaelic Studies* 9, 116-27.
1962*
"*Barp* and *Hvarf*", in *Scottish Gaelic Studies* 9, 131-35.
1976
"Scandinavian Place-Names in Ireland", in *Proceedings of the Seventh Viking Congress* (Held in Dublin, 15.-21. August, 1973), ed. by Almqvist, Bo, and Greene, D., RIA, Dublin, 125-33.
Óla, Árni,
1979
Landnámið fyrir landnám Reykjavík.
Olsen, M.,
1933
"Fra Hávamál til Krákumál", in *Festskrift til Halvdan Koht på sekstiårsdagen* Oslo, 93-102 (repr. in *Norrøne Studier* Oslo, 1938, 236-44).
Pálsson, Hermann,
1962
"Forfeður Erplinga", in *Íslenzk tunga* 3 (1961-62), 66-69.
Pálsson, Jens,
1978
"Some Anthropological Characteristics of Icelanders Analyzed with Regard to the Problem of Ethnogenesis", in *Journal of Human Evolution* 7, 695-702.
Pedersen H,.
1900
"Mandjævning hos Kelterne", in *Festskrift til J.L. Ussing* Copenhagen, 187-92.
Pokorny, J.,
1921
"Germanisch-Irisches", in *Zeitschrift für celtische Philologie* 13, 111-29.
Sawyer, P.H.,
1969
"The Two Viking Ages of Britain: A Discussion", in *Mediaeval Scandinavia* 2, 163-76.
1982
"The Causes of the Viking Age", in *The Vikings* ed. by Farrell, R.T., Phillimore & Co. Ltd., London and Chichester, 1-7.
1982*
"The Vikings and Ireland", in *Ireland in Early Mediaeval Europe* ed. by Whitelock, D., McKitterick, R., and Dumville, D., Cambridge University Press, 345-61.

Smyth, A.P.,
1972
"The Earliest Irish Annals: Their First Contemporary Entries, and the Earliest Centres of Recording", in *Proceedings of RIA* 72 C, 1-48.
1975/1979
Scandinavian York and Dublin I-II, Dublin.
1976
"The Black Foreigners of York and the White Foreigners of Dublin", in *Saga-Book* 19, 101-117.

Sommerfelt, A.,
1917
"Traditioner om Skandinaverne i Nordvest-Donegal", in *Maal og Minne* 153-55.
1950
"The Norsemen in Present Day Donegal Tradition", in *Journal of Celtic Studies* 1, 232-38.
1952
"Norse-Gaelic Contacts", in *Norsk Tidsskrift for Sprogvidenskap* 16, 226-36 (also further notes: 375-76).
1954
"Et Låneord fra Gaelisk", in *Maal og Minne* 197-99.

Stokes, W.,
1878
"On the Gaelic Names in the Landnámabók and Runic Inscriptions", in *Revue Celtique* 3 (1876-78), 186-91.
1885
"A few Parallels between the Old-Norse and the Irish Literatures and Traditions", in *Arkiv för nordisk Filologi* 2, 339-41.

Sveinsson, Einar Ólafur,
1945
Landnám í Skaftafellsþingi Reykjavík.
1952
"Vísa í Hávamálum og írsk saga", in *Skírnir* 126, 168-77.
1960
"Samtíningur", in *Skírnir* 134, 187-99.

von Sydow, C.W:,
1934
"Nibelungendiktningen och sägnen om "An bheoir lochlannach"", in *Studia Germanica, tillägnade E.A. Kock* Lund, 377-84.

Taylor, A.B.,
1958
"Dumazbakki — an Irish Place Name in Old Norse Form", in *Journal of the Royal Society of Antiquaries of Ireland* 88, 111-14.

1968
"The Norsemen in St. Kilda", in *Saga-Book* 17 (1967-68), 116-44.
Thomson, R.L.,
1963
"Scottish Gaelic *ucas, ucsa* Once More", in *Scottish Gaelic Studies* 10, 62-68.
Tveitane, M.,
1966
"Irish Apochrypha in Norse Tradition? On the Sources of some Medieval Homilies", in *Arv* 22, 111-35.
Víkingur, Sveinn,
1970
Getið í eyður sögunnar Kvöldvökuútgáfan.
de Vries, J,.
1957
"Les rapports des poésies Scaldique et Gaëlique", in *Ogam* 9, 13-26.
1965
"Germanic and Celtic Heroic Traditions", in *Saga-Book* 16 (1962-65), 22-40.
1965*
"Celtic and Germanic Religion", in *Saga-Book* 16 (1962-65). 109-23.
Wamers, E.,
1983
"Some Ecclesiastical and Secular Insular Metalwork Found in Norwegian Viking Graves", in *Peritia* 2, 277-306.
Wilde, W.,
1869
"On the Scandinavian Antiquities lately Discovered at Islandsbridge, near Dublin", in *Proceedings of RIA* 10 (1866-69), 13-22.
Young, J.I.,
1934
"Olaf Peacock's Journey to Ireland", in *Acta Philologica Scandinavica* 8 (1933-34), 94-96.
Þorsteinsson, Björn,
1965
"Hlutur Kelta í landnámi Íslands", in *Tímarit Máls og menningar* 26, 352-61.

INDEX OF TEXTS,
AUTHORS AND CRITICS

157

162

INDEX OF CHARACTERS
AND PLACES

STUDIA ISLANDICA
ÍSLENSK FRÆÐI

171

19. *Tvær ritgerðir um kveðskap Stephans G. Stephanssonar.*
Óskar Ó. Halldórsson: *Á ferð og flugi.*
Sigurður V. Friðþjófsson: *Kolbeinslag* (1961)
20. Peter Hallberg: *Snorri Sturluson och Egils saga Skallagrímssonar.* Ett
försök till språklig författarbestämning (1962)
21. Ólafur Briem: *Vanir og Æsir* (1963)
22. Peter Hallberg: *Ólafr Þórðarson hvítaskáld, Knýtlinga saga och Laxdæla saga.* Ett försök till språklig författarbestämning (1963)
23. Björn Guðfinnsson: *Um íslenzkan framburð. Mállýzkur II.*
Ólafur M. Ólafsson og Óskar Ó. Halldórsson unnu úr gögnum höf-
undar og bjuggu til prentunar (1964)
24. Ólafur Halldórsson: *Helgafellsbækur fornar* (1966)
25. Anthony Faulkes: *Rauðúlfs þáttr. A Study* (1966)
26. Helgi Guðmundsson: *Um Kjalnesinga sögu. Nokkrar athuganir* (1967)
27. Þorleifur Hauksson: *Endurteknar myndir í kveðskap Bjarna
Thorarensens* (1968)
28. Páll Bjarnason: *Ástakveðskapur Bjarna Thorarensens og Jónasar
Hallgrímssonar* (1969)
29. Helga Kress: *Guðmundur Kamban. Æskuverk og ádeilur* (1970)
30. Hermann Pálsson and Paul Edwards: *Legendary fiction in medieval
Iceland* (1971)
31. Grímur Thomsen: *On the Character of the Old Northern Poetry.*
Edited and introduced by Edward J. Cowan and Hermann Pálsson. –
Edward J. Cowan: *Icelandic Studies in Eighteenth and Nineteenth
Century Scotland* (1972)
32. Helgi Skúli Kjartansson: *Myndmál Passíusálmanna og aðrar
athuganir um stíl* (1973)
33. Davíð Erlingsson: *Blómað mál í rímum.*
Sveinn Skorri Höskuldsson: *In memoriam. Dr. phil. Steingrímur J.
Þorsteinsson, prófessor.*
Einar Sigurðsson: *Ritaskrá Steingríms J. Þorsteinssonar* (1974)
34. Einar Ól. Sveinsson: *Löng er för. – Þrír þættir um írskar og
íslenzkar sögur og kvæði* (1975)
35. Silja Aðalsteinsdóttir: *Þjóðfélagsmynd íslenskra barnabóka. –
Athugun á barnabókum íslenskra höfunda á árunum 1960–70* (1976)
36. Richard Perkins: *Flóamanna saga, Gaulverjabær and Haukr Erlends-
son* (1978)
37. Bjarni Guðnason: *Fyrsta sagan* (1978)
38. Fríða Á. Sigurðardóttir: *Leikrit Jökuls Jakobssonar* (1980)
39. Hermann Pálsson: *Úr hugmyndaheimi Hrafnkels sögu og Grettlu*
(1981)
40. Ólafur Jónsson: *Bækur og lesendur. – Um lestrarvenjur* (1982)

172